The Body in Jean-Luc Godard's New Wave Films

This original study examines the representation of the body in French New Wave films through discussion of a series of films by Jean-Luc Godard, perhaps the central figure of the French New Wave.

Through analysis of *À bout de souffle*, *Une femme est une femme*, *Le Mépris* and *Alphaville*, alongside discussion of some of Godard's lesser-known French New Wave films, the book explores the interrelation between bodies, books and bathrooms that they facilitate. In so doing, it aims to destabilise the French New Wave's myth of male exceptionalism and denaturalise the gender dynamic most commonly viewed at its heart, revealing that the women who make up a fundamental part of its fabric are not textually trapped by Godard's authorial presence. Instead, their corporeality disrupts any purported authorial and national ownership of their bodies.

Given the enduring popularity and visibility of the French New Wave, and of Jean-Luc Godard, in universities and journals, *The Body in Jean-Luc Godard's New Wave Films* will appeal to scholars in the disciplines of French and film studies, as well as to undergraduate and postgraduate students of these disciplines.

Francesca Minnie Hardy is Senior Lecturer in Film and Television at Nottingham Trent University. Her research explores the body's relationship to cinema, both on- and off-screen. Her first monograph, titled *Vital Resonances: Encountering Film with Varda, Haneke and Nancy*, was published in 2021 by Edinburgh University Press.

Routledge Focus on Film Studies

Weimar Cinema, Embodiment, and Historicity
Cultural Memory and the Historical Films of Ernst Lubitsch
Mason Kamana Allred

Migrants in Contemporary Spanish Film
Clara Guillén Marín

Virtue and Vice in Popular Film
Joseph H. Kupfer

Unproduction Studies and the American Film Industry
James Fenwick

Indian Indies
A Guide to New Independent Indian Cinema
Ashvin Immanuel Devasundaram

Migration and Identity in British East and Southeast Asian Cinema
Leung Wing-Fai

Con Artists in Cinema
Self-Knowledge, Female Power, and Love
Joseph H. Kupfer

The Body in Jean-Luc Godard's New Wave Films
Francesca Minnie Hardy

For more information about this series, please visit: https://www.routledge.com/Routledge-Focus-on-Film-Studies/book-series/RFFS

The Body in Jean-Luc Godard's New Wave Films

Francesca Minnie Hardy

LONDON AND NEW YORK

First published 2024
by Routledge
4 Park Square, Milton Park, Abingdon, Oxon OX14 4RN

and by Routledge
605 Third Avenue, New York, NY 10158

Routledge is an imprint of the Taylor & Francis Group, an informa business

© 2024 Francesca Minnie Hardy

The right of Francesca Minnie Hardy to be identified as author of this work has been asserted in accordance with sections 77 and 78 of the Copyright, Designs and Patents Act 1988.

All rights reserved. No part of this book may be reprinted or reproduced or utilised in any form or by any electronic, mechanical, or other means, now known or hereafter invented, including photocopying and recording, or in any information storage or retrieval system, without permission in writing from the publishers.

Trademark notice: Product or corporate names may be trademarks or registered trademarks, and are used only for identification and explanation without intent to infringe.

British Library Cataloguing-in-Publication Data
A catalogue record for this book is available from the British Library

ISBN: 978-1-032-23203-4 (hbk)
ISBN: 978-1-032-23204-1 (pbk)
ISBN: 978-1-003-27624-1 (ebk)

DOI: 10.4324/9781003276241

Typeset in Times New Roman
by codeMantra

In loving memory of June and Dennis Robinson,
aka nan and grandad.

Contents

	Acknowledgements	*ix*
1	Introduction	1
2	The art cinema body in theory	7
3	Lingering in the men's room	19
4	Of aliens and alter egos	29
5	Of bathroom sinks and the streets below	41
6	Of wigs and fig leaves	53
7	Of totalitarianism and toilet doors	63
8	Conclusion	76
	Index	*81*

Acknowledgements

My initial thanks must go to Doug Morrey who suggested that I write an article on the French New Wave as part of a special edition of *Studies in French Cinema* (now *French Screen Studies*) he was guest editing. It's safe to say that the article got away from me, and the result is this book. Doug, any future pints at The Queen Vic in the Deen are on me.

Thank you also to Kelly O'Brien, Natalie Foster and Jen Vennall at Routledge for being so communicative and supportive. You made delivery of the book painless.

I'm also grateful to friends and colleagues at Nottingham Trent University—Cüneyt Çakirlar, Laura Coffey-Glover, Simon Cross, Anna Dawson, Sophie Fuggle, Steve Jones, Martin O'Shaughnessy, Ben Taylor, Jamie Williams and Dave Woods—for the good humour and distractions they always offer. *Nolite te bastardes carborundorum.*

My final thanks, as ever, to Rory Waterman and to mum, dad and Jenny.

1 Introduction

Writing on Europe's only 'indigenous' (Fowler 2002, 9) genre, Steve Neale deems the body a key vehicle for art cinema's distinction from Hollywood. He describes these representations as inscriptions, incisive impressions which attend to questions regarding performance and actors, to the choice of bodies onscreen, and to the tones and textures they produce. Neale goes on to enumerate the strains of this inscription in a series of European art cinemas and binds them to questions of rhetoric and refusal. German Expressionism, he writes, 'stresses the rhetoric of bodily movement and gesture' (1981, 31), most famously inscribed by the aberrant, angular body of somnambulist Cesare in *Das Cabinet des Dr Caligari* (Robert Wiene 1920). Soviet cinema, he notes, is 'marked by a refusal of the star system' and, alongside Italian Neo-realism, the 'use of non-professional actors' whose 'untrained bodies' (de Luca 2014, 32) foster singular textures which, through their amateurishness, admit access to a 'spontaneous real' (75–7). At the opposite end of this textural spectrum, Federico Fellini 'construct[s] an "over-inscription" of the fetishised body of the star [...] through a rhetoric of systematic hyperbole' (Neale 1981, 31). Frolicking in the waters of the Trevi Fountain, Anita Ekberg is a marker of insincere excess. Across Neale's taxonomy, then, the body is a verb. Its inscription does things to the profilmic.

Conspicuously absent from Neale's catalogue of art cinema corporeality, however, is the French New Wave, and we might be satisfied to plug this gap by allying its own corporeal inscriptions with the rhetoric and refusals cited above. Yet the French New Wave's orthodoxy of non-professionalism, of which the untrained, amateur body is a principal vessel, compounds Neale's omission (Vincendeau 2000, 110). Indeed, it is surprising that no prior book has been written about the body in French New Wave film. This is a strange omission given that some of its most iconic sequences are built around the body, around bodily events, around the pleasures of the flesh, of being a body. Running with abandon, the lungs full of air and the muscles full of lactic acid, making love, smoking: we have all likely been (perhaps now guiltily) seduced by such sequences, attempted their feats, bought their T-shirts. Such bodily

2 Introduction

pleasures are perhaps best emblematised by Franz, Arthur, and Odile's sprint through the Louvre in *Bande à part* (Jean-Luc Godard 1964), which Agnès Varda, among countless others, playfully recreates in her recent collaboration with visual artist JR, *Visages, Villages* (2017) (Figures 1.1 and 1.2).

Figure 1.1 Franz, Arthur and Odile sprinting through the Louvre in *Bande à part* (1964).

Figure 1.2 Agnès Varda and JR sprinting through the Louvre in *Visages, Villages* (2017).

Varda's iteration operates as a potted history of French New Wave bodies: an imitation of its fetish actors (here Sami Frey, Claude Brasseur and Anna Karina), an intensified *flânerie* and its stylistic impurity, '"irrigated" [...] by the "formidable resources" of its neighbouring arts' (Schmid 2019, 4), which Giuseppe Arcimboldo's seasonal portraits denote here and which in turn offer a condensed history of Varda's knotted French New Wave corporeality represented by the knotted faces in *La Pointe courte* (1955) and the knotted lovers' bodies in *L'Opéra-Mouffe* (1958) and *Le bonheur* (1965) (Figures 1.3 and 1.4). Most fundamentally, however, as we will come to see, Varda's (female) body destabilises the French New Wave's myth of male exceptionalism and what Geneviève Sellier terms 'cinema [...] in the first person masculine singular' (2008, 7). This is a cinematic conjugation that championed a 'personal cinema' (Sterritt 1999, 5) 'whose sensibilities were forged not within film schools [...] or studio apprenticeship systems [...] but within the private confines of [its directors'] own personalities' (6), and which in turn forged 'cultural schemas that privilege a narcissism and a desire for mastery that rework male domination in other forms' (Sellier 2008, 220). For instance, an imaginary museum which overwhelmingly celebrates male genius and indirectly rebukes the new opportunities available to women (see Lack 2018; Schmid 2019).

Figure 1.3 Varda's knotted French New Wave corporeality: *La Pointe courte* (1955).

4 *Introduction*

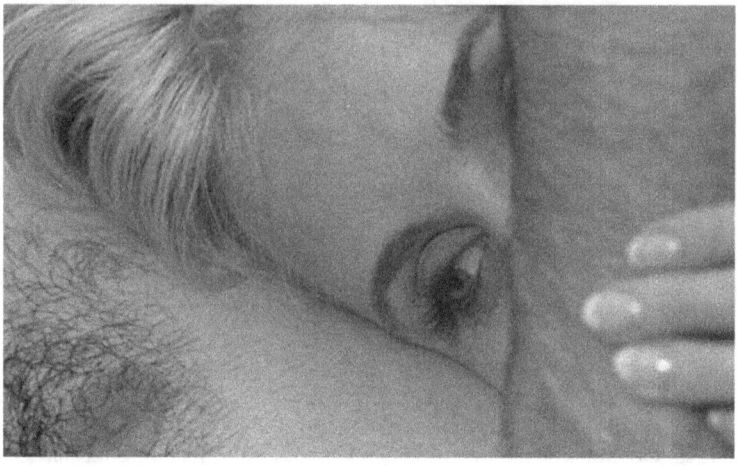

Figure 1.4 Varda's knotted French New Wave corporeality: *Le bonheur* (1965).

Such an omission is stranger still when one considers that the French New Wave loves a good book. In fact, it prides itself on being something of a bookworm, even an 'heir […] to a literary tradition' (Andrew 1988, 5), with books occupying an 'endemic (and nearly epidemic)' (Kline 1992, 3), and on occasion epistemic, status across French New Wave cinema (190). This hermeneutic triptych is especially true of the focus of this book, the French New Wave films of Jean-Luc Godard, whose 'reputation for using books as a prominent part of his mise-en-scène' (Hayes 2004, 32) aligns his early filmography with the 'repressed' (Kline 1992, 3) strain of literary adaption characteristic of this bookish film movement, whereby books materialise as 'object[s] of attention, and the bookstore as […] location of choice' (4). In *À bout de souffle* (1960), Michel Poiccard is a voracious reader, albeit of newspapers, whilst Émile, Franz, Ferdinand/Pierrot and Paul peruse Paris's bookshops in *Une femme est une femme* (1961), *Bande à part*, *Pierrot le fou* (1965) and *Masculin féminin* (1966), respectively. Significantly, in Godard's New Wave oeuvre, literature is not the preserve of the masculine: Anna Karina reads, or is read to, across her Godardian incarnations, perhaps most famously in *Vivre sa vie* (1962), and Jean Seberg and Brigitte Bardot are both resolute literary characters in their one-time collaborations with Godard. Although familiar to over half a century's worth of audiences, such literary practices also defamiliarize because they support Roland-François Lack's proposition 'that the French New Wave is less a cinema of *flânerie* than it is a cinema of stasis; is as much a cinema of interiors as it is a cinema of the street' (2018, 66). Reading, rather than walking, admits respite, and Godard's characters' penchant for reading in the bath (Ferdinand/Pierrot, Camille in *Le Mépris* [1963] and Corinne and Roland in *Week-end* [1967]) intensifies this stasis and ventures into the 'overlooked' (Baschiera 2020, 173) domestic spaces of the French New Wave where we will encounter some of the literary practices predominantly identified with the *salle de bain*, for example, meter readings and graffiti. Books thus occupy a prime position in the most body-conscious of rooms, the bathroom, seaming books, bodies and the bathroom together, a triptych that this book pursues.

How is it, then, that one of the most famous and influential cinematic movements of all time has failed to elicit such critical attention, considering there are bodies and bodies of work intimately associated with the French New Wave: *Les Cahiers du cinéma*, B.B., the young Turks, the players of *Les fiancés du pont Mac Donald* (Agnès Varda 1962)? Perhaps such debates have failed to ignite because the links between these bodies, as Vanessa R. Schwartz suggests, are thought to be too tenuous for sustained discussion, 'shar[ing] more by life circumstance [...] than they share as filmmakers' (2010, 146–7). After all, let us not forget that 'the term "nouvelle vague" was first used by Françoise Giroud in the pages of *L'Express* in 1957 [...] about the youthful postwar generation, it had nothing to do with the cinema' (146). It was, as Susan Hayward describes, 'a misnomer made myth' (2005, 231). Or perhaps, as James Tweedie contends, the fault lies not with the films' production context, but rather with their 'confining' (2013, 49) critical reception, which remains disproportionately attuned to the abovementioned private confines of directors' personalities, and consequently 'loses track of actual figures and actual carpets' (48–9). Nonetheless, there are actual bodies to behold. New bodies emerging, new material, lived realities taking hold during what Catherine Eades pregnantly calls a 'deliquescent climate' (2012, 114), a temperament readily taken up by New Wave filmmakers who sought to dissolve the stuffy *cinéma de papa* that came before them. There are thus bodies caught up in new waves of living, being, and becoming, a revolution famously satirised by Jacques Tati's body of work and the gradual incorporation of Hulot into his diegetic universe (Ross 1996, 176–7). Bodies, according to Antoine de Baecque (2006, 374), born in France but later made in the USA. Bodies descended from the essential quality of cinema: the recording of bodies in space and the telling of stories with them (371–2). This book therefore goes in search of the *nouvelle vague*'s missing *corps* and seeks to encourage sustained consideration of the body in French New Wave film—a carnal body made of bone, muscle, flesh, hair and the odd fake moustache.

References

Andrew, Dudley. 1988. *Breathless: Jean-Luc Godard, Director*. New Brunswick: Rutgers University Press.

Baschiera, Stefano. 2020. "At Home with the Nouvelle Vague: Apartment Plots and Domestic Urbanism in Godard's *Une femme est une femme* and Varda's *Cléo de 5 à 7*." In *Film and Domestic Space: Architectures, Representations, Dispositif*, edited by

Stefano Baschiera and Miriam de Rosa, 171–87. Edinburgh: Edinburgh University Press.
de Baecque, Antoine. 2006. "Le corps au cinéma." In *Histoire du corps: Les mutations du regard. Le XXe siècle*, edited by Jean-Jacques Courtine, 371–91. Paris: Seuil.
de Luca, Tiago. 2014. *Realism of the Senses in World Cinema: The Experience of Physical Reality*. London: I.B. Taurus.
Eades, Catherine. 2012. "Neorealism Another 'Cinéma de Papa' for the French New Wave?" In *Global Neorealism: The Transnational History of a Film Style*, edited by Saverio Giovacchini and Robert Sklar, 103–24. Jackson: University Press of Mississippi.
Fowler, Catherine. 2002. "Introduction." In *The European Cinema Reader*, edited by Catherine Fowler, 1–10. London: Routledge.
Hayes, Kevin. 2004. "The Body and the Book in *Contempt*." *Studies in European Cinema* 1 (1): 31–41.
Hayward, Susan. 2005. *French National Cinema* (Second Edition). Abingdon: Routledge.
Kline, T. Jefferson. 1992. *Screening the Text: Intertextuality in French New Wave Cinema*. Baltimore: The Johns Hopkins University Press.
Lack, Roland-François. 2018. "The New Wave Hotel." In *Paris in the Cinema: Beyond the Flâneur*, edited by Alastair Phillips and Ginette Vincendeau, 66–75. London: BFI Palgrave.
Neale, Steve. 1981. "Art Cinema as Institution." *Screen* 22 (1): 11–40.
Ross, Kristin. 1996. *Fast Cars, Clean Bodies: Decolonization and the Reordering of French Culture*. Cambridge, MA: The MIT Press.
Schmid, Marion. 2019. *Intermedial Dialogues: The French New Wave and the Other Arts*. Edinburgh: Edinburgh University Press.
Schwartz, Vanessa R. 2010. "Who Killed Brigitte Bardot? Perspectives on the New Wave at Fifty." *Cinema Journal* 49 (4): 145–52.
Sellier, Geneviève. 2008. *Masculine Singular: French New Wave Cinema*. Translated by Kristin Ross. Durham: Duke University Press.
Sterritt, David. 1999. *The Films of Jean-Luc Godard: Seeing the Invisible*. Cambridge: Cambridge University Press.
Tweedie, James. 2013. *The Age of New Waves: Art Cinema and the Staging of Globalization*. Oxford: Oxford University Press.
Vincendeau, Ginette. 2000. *Stars and Stardom in French Cinema*. London: Continuum.

2 The art cinema body in theory

For Gilles Deleuze, the French New Wave kindled new explorations of the body: 'since the new wave, every time there was a fine and powerful film, there was a new exploration of the body in it' (1989, 196). Here, however, he simultaneously appears to bracket out its bodies amongst these investigations. Ambiguously, it is only *since* the New Wave that these new explorations have transpired. Does this imply that a novel anatomy of the body in cinema has only taken place post the French New Wave? Significantly too, as Geneviève Sellier (2008) confirms, existing criticism has been very quiet on gender. Such critical inattention, then, could be allied to this exclusion, because these discussions often turn on questions of bodies, women's in particular, whose assumed aberrance in relation to the prescribed masculine norm inscribes them as other.

Like Anita Ekberg's prancing in the Trevi fountain, however, my original claim for silence may be a hyperbolic inscription, for the French New Wave body is not entirely unthought. Jean Douchet (1999) and Michel Marie (2003), in their respective surveys of the movement, both dedicate sections to the bodies that occupy New Wave screens, with Douchet calling it 'a physical cinema where movement becomes the center of interest' (1999, 153), and in which truth is sought 'in and through the body'—seemingly and uncritically found through preening: 'hard', he says, 'to think of Godard without thinking of the way his female characters are always combing their hair or of the incessant sensual movements of their heads' (151; see also Loshitzky 1995). Whilst for Marie (2003, 113), New Wave embodiment enjoys a certain dynastic tendency, or typage, where an individuated, fetishistic strain replaces the traditional moral and sociopolitical mobilisation of physiognomy. Such faces that overwhelmingly 'belonged to Jean-Paul Belmondo and Jean-Pierre Léaud' (114), as well as to Jeanne Moreau, are representative of the French New Wave itself:

it is for *Jules and Jim*'s Catherine, Truffaut's richest and more polymorphous character, that Jeanne Moreau assembles all of Truffaut's feminine figures: wife and mistress, she will alternately resemble Lena, Therese, Colette, Nicole, Linda, and Clarisse, Julie Kohler, Christine, and Marion.

8 The art cinema body in theory

They are all nothing more than the different facets of the heroine Catherine, from *Jules and Jim*.

(125)

Similarly, de Baecque (2006, 384–5) identifies the French New Wave as the kernel of corporeal truth—a truth engendered by Brigitte Bardot in particular and the films' escape from the material trappings of the studio in general. Indeed, misogynistic asides aside, such as Godard's vicarious proclamation in *Le Mépris* (1963) that you show a woman a camera and she'll show you her ass, according to existing accounts, the French New Wave's paradigmatic body is a (wandering) female one, and, as if in response to Sellier, Mark Betz's expansive undertaking of these perambulations ties these bodies intimately to the film's body.

The pace of her flânerie is the pace of the art film itself; the visual shocks she encounters are the shock cuts punctuating and structuring narrative sequences, she is the visualizing subject. But she is also an object in the narrative and in the landscapes and architectures she traverses.

(2009, 95)

Betz's prepositional iteration recalls Neale's inscription, and the on-screen body once again precipitates as verb; it does things to the profilmic, the latter's rhythm, and ruptures contiguous with the profilmic female figure. Betz's thesis attributes an exciting primacy to women's bodies, and we might think of Agnès Varda's *Cléo de 5 à 7* (1962) and its expert elaboration of the labour that goes into being a (female) body in the world. This overt admission of labour, its exposure for all to see and hear, as the sound, for example, of footsteps produced by feet squeezed into high heels clip-clopping on the Parisian pavement, and its subsequent dismantling, contributes to *Cléo de 5 à 7* being a remarkable film and Varda a remarkable figure amongst the French New Wave. Long recognised as the only female filmmaker of this period, with the usual caveats, she is also one of the few directors to address the body *qua* corporeality, the body as involving bodywork, a fleshy appreciation she anticipates, and admittedly sanitises, in the later film, in her Surrealist short *L'Opéra-Mouffe* (1958).[1] Through visual metaphor and montage, the body here squirms with an at times frightening vitality. A swollen, pregnant belly, for instance, is likened to a rotund pumpkin that is violently scraped clean of its seeds. In what was then one of Paris's poorest *quartiers*, the streets of La Mouffe reveal the body to be verb.

These wanderings are reminiscent of Deleuze's post-war cinematic 'seers' (1989, 41) who traipse across Europe's ruined landscapes. Beyond these wanderings, like Betz, Deleuze gives a delightful account of the body in French

New Wave film—perhaps why it has largely been avoided *since*—designating it the 'cinema of bodies' (193):

> The new wave, in France, has taken this cinema of attitudes and postures [...] a long way. [...] Embracing, striking, intertwining and bumping bodies animate major scenes [...]. The body is sound as well as visible. All the components of the image come together on the body.

The body here is verb: it animates. Embracing, striking, intertwining and bumping bodies populate these New Wave worlds. Embracing, striking, intertwining and bumping, these New Wave bodies create a world through their frictions, collisions and caresses, their proximity. Bodily matter produces cinema. Indeed, the body here is presented as the underlying structure of the image. Its acoustic, visual, and kinesthetic registers coalesce on the body. Significantly, however, these bodies are not immaculate, and Deleuze traces their genealogy in the cinema of John Cassavetes. Paraphrasing the director, Deleuze notes how 'characters must not come from a story or plot, but that the story should be secreted by the characters [...]: the character is reduced to his own bodily attitudes, and what ought to result is the gest' (192). Again, the body here is verb: it secretes. But what do these bodies secrete? Deleuze unwittingly hints at a messier, more visceral reduction than one of attitudes alone. Still discussing Cassavetes, he notes how '[e]very time, space is made up of these excrescences of body' (193) *inter alia*. Secretions are thus figured as excrescences. Bodily matter becomes bodily excess, and as an inheritor of this bodily treatment, the French New Wave becomes a cinema of bodily excess in spite of its own '"clean-slate" policy' (Vincendeau 2000, 6).

In a sociopolitical context, this is a strange discourse because, emerging towards the middle of *les trente glorieuses* (1945–75), the French New Wave burgeoned as France fervently began to embrace the cult of cleanliness. Just as French society was cleaning home and body, its cinema was getting messy. Nevertheless, and reflective of the sanitary zeitgeist, the vernacular attached to the French New Wave highlights its hygienic properties. It came out of '[t]he era of purification and revitalization of the [French] film industry' (Neupert 2007, 5), which in turn needed 'desanitising' (Hayward 2005, 206) by the French New Wave, which in turn, and in the wake of Roland Barthes' analysis of soap powders and detergents in *Mythologies* (1972 [1957]), was, according to Claude Chabrol, 'promoted like a new brand of soap' (quoted in Neupert 2007, 3). Kristin Ross offers the definitive account of this period and reads 'the story of French modernization and Americanization' (1996, 7) and that of decolonisation as Deleuze does French New Wave corporeality: as embracing, striking, intertwining and bumping bodies, an animation which produces tension, collaboration and/or fusion. Cinema, both Hollywood and national, as Ross's peerless intervention shows, is intimately caught up with this period, effectively purveying lifestyle directives veiled as choices. More proximate still is the relationship between cinema and the objects of this sparklingly new world. The interrelationship between cars and cinema, for instance, has been richly detailed, and Ross deftly articulates how cinema organises object 'social relations' (90) on both sides of the screen: *mise en scène* merges with social mandate. Objects as props orchestrate comportment on-screen, where these 'common objects' (149) become didactic, 'assertive' (38), endorsing new behaviour off-screen, eventually coming to fill the homes of the new French middle class, and ultimately neutralising into prosaic props once more. *L'Ascenseur pour l'échafaud* (Louis Malle, 1958) is instructive here. For, whilst Ross understands the alien properties of the gun as Julien's downfall, it is the film's opening shot which dampened interest in French New Wave bodies: Jeanne Moreau in close-up.

In *Masculine Singular* Sellier considers the 'new sensuality' (2008, 186) that this shot crystallises, which, as Vincendeau summarises, 'was [...] at the centre of the shift in the representation of female eroticism from the body to the face' (2000, 125). What does this cephalic body secrete, then? Nationhood. A history of women's heads in twentieth- and early twenty-first-century France, from *les tondues* to *les femmes voilées*, as Alison Moore has shown, illustrates this coincidence. For example, Moore highlights how 'women's heads' (2005, 677) have acted 'as the locus of contested nationhood' through the misuse of 'photographs of veiled Islamic women [...] throughout the 1990s to promote associations of the veil with the threat of violence imputed to Islamic fundamentalism'. She continues:

> Here again gender acts as a vehicle for a politics that is invoked not (or not only) by verbal assertion but by visual repetition. [...] Representation of the headscarves debate shows that women's bodies remain a question of national self-definition in France, and that gendered visuality is a persistent medium through which to assert a politics that might hold less power if forced to articulate itself only verbally.

In this way, the French New Wave's novel and cephalic sensuality, which libidinally cathects women's heads via the close-up, furthers Moore's thesis by adding another installment to this narrative, whilst it extends Neale's thinking on 'the marks of nationality' that art cinema retains, and indeed encourages, when operating as national cinema, and that 'serve [...] to differentiate [it] from the films produced in Hollywood' (1981, 34–5). These distinguishing marks thus form the hinge between a film's national identity and its 'international circulation' (35), and while Neale gives the more obvious mark of dialogue as an example of such affiliation, French New Wave films inadvertently construct and reconstruct French national identity by means of the shift in the representation of female eroticism they enact and the gendered visuality the role of the close-up plays in this shift to make up yet another instance of the collapse Moore tracks between women's heads and French national identity, and thereby produce another distinguishing mark that once again centres on the body.

Godard's New Wave period, however, complicates such distinguishing marks owing to one of his 'trademarks' (Loshitzky 1995, 138): his 'attraction for non-French actresses' (137–8). When shot in close-up, Jean Seberg and Anna Karina embody this distinguishing mark, yet as the visual and verbal coalesce, their accented French, and occasional misunderstandings, set up a subtle conflict with Godard and the first-person masculine singular frequently associated with the French New Wave by eroding the stabilising effects produced by the director's name (see Betz 2009, 68). According to Betz, '[w]hen confronted with the evidence of multinational investment in an art film, authorship picks up the slack' (69) by anchoring a film to stable national and cinematic identities, and whilst any sense of the multinational here predominantly concerns performance, the bodies of Seberg and Karina (and others) discreetly unmoor Godard's cinema from these stable contexts, which elsewhere he seeks to contain via the conceit of the film-within-a-film, for example, in *Le Mépris* and *Masculin féminin* (1966). After all, the body is audible as well as visible, and this erosion signals a perhaps unexpected sense of female agency in Godard's New Wave films that 'undo[es] and rework[s] the codes that embed male subjectivity into film narratives' (Ince 2017, 49). Such agency counters the triptych that typically shapes Godard's on-screen women which equates them with sexuality (Morrey 2005, 10; see also Mulvey and MacCabe 1980), punishes them with death (Morrey 2005, 27) and/or diminishes their credibility (57). Such qualities make any 'cries […] for a feminist reinterpretation' (Loshitzky 1995, 135) of Godard's work hard to reckon with, yet the ability to periodise different eras of his career with reference to different female collaborators both on- and off-screen softens this position somewhat and contributes to the feminist strategy that 'seeks to reclaim female agency within dominant discourses rather than merely viewing those discourses as oppressive' (Chaudhuri 2006, 62). Something of a double bind of impunity and complicity thus embroils Godard's images of women during much of his New Wave oeuvre (and beyond) (Mulvey and MacCabe 1980, 101), which simultaneously critiques and extends suspect representations of women on-screen (87). Further indicative of this double bind, the erosion of the French New Wave's cephalic-centred nationalism ultimately becomes a Godardian impulse when in the closing moments of *Week-end* (1967), and arguably in the final moments of his New Wave period, Corinne (Mireille Drac), one half of the film's scheming husband and wife team who lead us through its apocalyptic pastoral cannibalises Roland (Jean Yanne), in close-up, and in so doing cannibalises one of the New Wave's key eroticising tools. 'Maybe I'll have more later', she says. It was to be ten years before Godard returned to narrative cinema.

What else does this cephalic body secrete? Most obviously, it secretes the face, the face in close-up, somehow limiting, even sanitising, the body's secretions. The close-up, however, does offer a privileged site from which to consider corporeal excess, as Mary Ann Doane demonstrates. Like Deleuze, Doane traces a genealogy of the close-up look on the world that cinema can offer and starts with the anatomical tragedy of Jean Epstein's *photogénie*:

> I will never find the way to say how I love American close-ups. Point blank. A head suddenly appears on screen and drama, now face to face, seems to address me personally and swells with an extraordinary intensity. I am hypnotized. Now the tragedy is anatomical. The decor of the fifth act is this corner of a cheek torn by a smile. [...] The orography of the face vacillates. Seismic shocks begin. Capillary wrinkles try to split the fault. A wave carries them away. Crescendo. A muscle bridles. The lip is laced with tics like a theater curtain. [...] Crack. The mouth gives way, like a ripe fruit splitting open. As if slit by a scalpel, a keyboard-like smile cuts laterally into the corner of the lips.
>
> (2003, 89–90)

Everything here is in slow motion. The verbal becomes cinematic. This is a close-up shot of a face, which materialises as full of seams: tears, cracks, splits, slits, cuts, lips, from which the body spills out, secretes. The body is sound—crescendo—as well as vision—crack. Epstein's prose here is startling, and Doane's response is no less so:

> The description verges on the obscene, perhaps because it transforms the face, usually reserved as the very locus of subjectivity, into a series of harsh and alien objects [...]. The excessiveness of Epstein's language is consistent with the inescapably hyperbolic nature of the close-up. [...] But in addition, Epstein's prose extracts and abstracts the close-up from the scene, from the body, from the spatiotemporal coordinates of the narrative, performing, in effect, its monstrosity. Any viewer is invited to examine its gigantic detail, its contingencies, its idiosyncrasies.
>
> (90)

Hyperbolic, monstrous, gigantic, the close-up mutates the body, specifically the face, into an obscene and alien object world, simultaneously excess and detail; it also enacts violence, tearing the body apart, as well as its contents from the film proper. According to Martine Beugnet, these rents 'endow[...] the close-up with a force of *interpellation*: it insists, calls on and directs the attention of the viewer. [...] (forcibly) bring[ing] the eye where it would not normally look' (2006, 25; original emphasis). Beugnet, however, departs from the thingliness of Doane's conception of the close-up by stressing how these 'uncanny intimacies' transform the body into 'an organic mass', into 'matter'. Thingly and organic, excess and detail, the close-up seams contradictions.

Karl Schoonover pursues this seam in his work on the body in Italian Neorealism. Here the whole body, rather than the face alone, is excess—'the body at risk, in pain, or injured' (2012, 19)—and detail—'markings, postures, gestures, tics, or facial expressions'. Via Bazin, Schoonover offers an almost schematic understanding of cinematic corporeality. The body is obscene, pornographic; it overwhelms the spectator (1). The body marks the image with 'an exorbitant visuality' (2). The body is 'a ledger of the real'. The body, like the close-up, promises contingency (4). Once again, bodily matter produces cinema. The body here is verb; it does things to the profilmic:

> Bazin's fascination with particular gaits, characteristic gestures, injury, and scars is in this sense not just about the inscription of a document. It is also about the storage and transport of a body: through cinema the body gains transfer to other times and spaces. But not only does the cinematic image move the body; the body also moves the image.
>
> (21)

Schoonover here returns us to where we began: inscription and animation. The body becomes a mark, a stain, a secretion, an excrescence that moves, establishing something of an anti-hygienist yet humanist ontology of cinematic corporeality. The brutalised, suffering, imperiled, injured bodies that populate Italian neorealist films, and Schoonover's thinking, are not necessarily redolent of the French New Wave. This, in part at least, might be attributable to the censorship that presided over the French film industry during this time (see Dine 1994, 218–22; Greene 1999, 9 and 35; Sharpe 2017, 130) with any film that tackled 'the Algerian question' (Betz 2009, 102–4), and the obvious issue of torture this period entails, especially vulnerable to censure. Testimonies attest to the use of domestic spaces as places of torture whereby, as Ross details, '[t]he dark underside of French comfort emerges' (1996, 111). 'The new techniques that were revolutionizing' the space of the home, Ross continues, 'were putting a modern, more hygienic touch on torture as well' (113). Michel Subor handcuffed to a bathtub in *Le Petit Soldat* (1960) literalises this seam between torture and hygiene. Jean-Paul Belmondo's waterboarding in *Pierrot le fou* satirises it (Figures 2.1 and 2.2).

The bathroom thus facilitates a permissible sidelong glance at the present, whilst telescoping back in time, for in the aftermath of the Holocaust the shower is a 'permanently contaminated' (Higgins 1996, 15), 'historically overdetermined image' (16). In this way, the bathroom encompasses France's '*during*-war period' (Feldman 2014, 2; original emphasis), and prosaic props become sociopolitically resonant once more.

Doubtless, though, the French New Wave possesses its own prescribed corporeal schema. Women's faces, as we have seen, are subbed in for the rest of the body and subsequently cathected with libidinal desires and nationhood. We might thus add frontality to this schema, a corporeal and significantly a cephalic visual economy that 'is aimed at maximizing the expressivity and

14 The art cinema body in theory

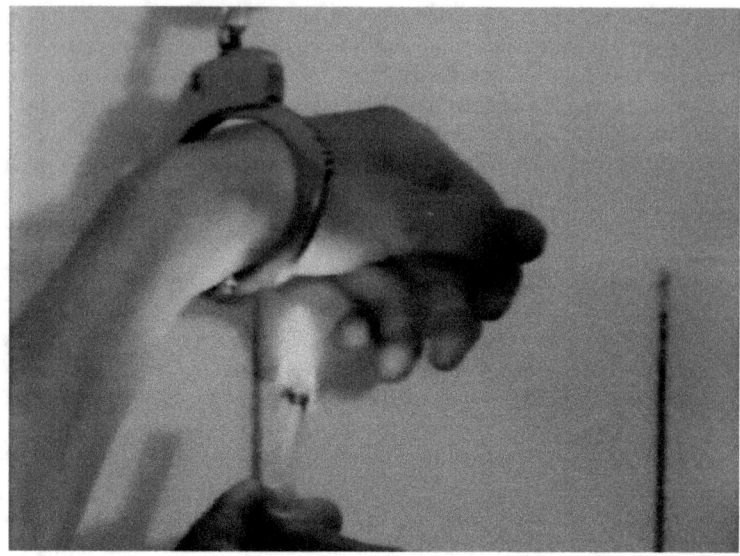

Figure 2.1 Michel Subor handcuffed to a bathtub in *Le Petit Soldat* (1960).

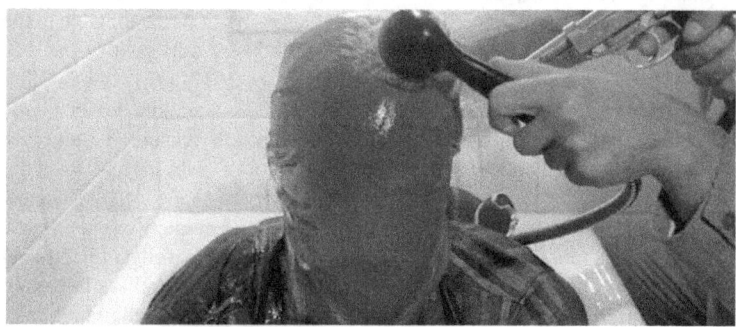

Figure 2.2 Jean-Paul Belmondo being waterboarded in *Pierrot le fou* (1965).

psychological/emotional intelligibility of a film for the viewer' (Colvin 2017, 191) with three of the five 'behavioral cues' (192) associated with this *mise en scène* centred on the face. Thus, the body is subordinated to 'mental states' and the mind, whilst it is further displaced through the institutionalised understatement of New Wave style which celebrates authenticity, naturalism, spontaneity and improvisation, but which is contemporaneous with a concentration 'on behaviour, looks and gestures rather than psychology' (Vincendeau 2000, 117). As such, the French New Wave body meets the requirements of

Deleuze's cinema of bodies, for these behaviours, looks and gestures ostensibly secrete a story: bodily matter produces cinema. Yet, in a critical context at least, the body disappears behind this schematic understatement, and we witness something similar in Marion Schmid's work on intermediality and the French New Wave. '[O]rganised [...] as a series of interfaces between cinema and one of its sister arts' (2019, 5)—literature, theatre, painting, architecture and photography—'where media rivalries, encounters and hybridisations are [...] enacted' (5), here corporeality endures as a secondary critical concern even though the body often realises the movement's legitimating intermedial impurity (4). For instance, the painterly resonances of the geometric, bodily abstractions that transform walls and bedsheets into canvases to be filled in Godard's *Une femme mariée* (1964) (110) or Varda's ludic recreation of two Pablo Picasso etchings in *Lion's Love* (1969) (102–4). In both instances, the body's *mise en scène* produces a *mise en scène* that gives rise to intermediality; nonetheless, the body becomes a critical spectre. A return to the Louvre demonstrates as much:

> If the Louvre sequence literally and metaphorically puts painting in its place – that of the museum, but also of an ancestor surpassed by a more vibrant younger sibling – its revisiting of works of the past raises fundamental questions about the different ontologies of cinema and painting, the relation between tradition and modernity, and the renewal of aesthetic canons.
>
> (94)

Fundamentally, Schmid's reading absents the body from the film's *mise en scène*. The sprinting bodies of Frey, Brasseur and Karina barely even haunt the halls of the Louvre here, and in this way, Schmid offers an 'abridged' history of critical interventions into French New Wave corporeality and risks upholding the masculine singular. Nevertheless, the body here is verb; it does things to the profilmic.

Across a series of contexts, then, New Wave bodies are displaced, and whilst we are likelier to find the New Wave body at leisure—or 'in bed' (Betz 2009, 104), as Godard lamented—than at risk, a leisurely body possesses a corporeality, to which New Wave films attest. It is such 'inoccupation of bodies' (Barthes 1989, 346), moreover, that Barthes understands as constitutive of 'modern eroticism', which he explicitly ties to the space of the cinema and which Godard lampoons in *Les Carabiniers* (1963) when Michelangelo (Albert Juross) attempts to enter the screen and share a bath no less with the blonde on-screen (Figure 2.3). We will see this leisurely corporeality on display in the bathrooms of a series of New Wave films by Godard, who, contra the presiding sociocultural hygienist tone of *les trentes glorieuses*, famously made a mess of his first feature film (Nowell-Smith 2008, 196) and concluded his New Wave period with a film found on a scrap heap.

16 *The art cinema body in theory*

Figure 2.3 Michelangelo (Albert Juross) in *Les Carabiniers* (1963) attempts to enter the screen and share a bath with the blonde on-screen.

Note

1 These caveats concern Varda's first feature film, *La Pointe courte* (1955), which, shot five years before the directorial debuts of Chabrol, Godard and Truffaut, anticipated a series of the stylistic tropes of the French New Wave (see Vincendeau 2008), and Marguerite Duras's screenplay for Alain Resnais's *Hiroshima mon amour* (1959).

References

Barthes, Roland. 1989. *The Rustle of Language*. Translated by Richard Howard. New York: Hill and Wang.

Barthes, Roland. 1972 [1957]. *Mythologies*. Translated by Annette Lavers. New York: The Noonday Press.

Betz, Mark. 2009. *Beyond the Subtitle: Remapping European Cinema*. Minneapolis: University of Minnesota Press.

Beugnet, Martine. 2006. "Close-up Vision: Re-mapping the Body in the Work of Contemporary French Women Filmmakers." *Nottingham French Studies* 45 (3): 24–38.

Chaudhuri, Shohini. 2006. *Feminist Film Theorists: Laura Mulvey, Kaja Silverman, Teresa de Lauretis, Barbara Creed*. London: Routledge.

Colvin, J. Brandon. 2017. "The Other Side of Frontality: Dorsality in European Art Cinema." *New Review of Film and Television Studies* 15 (2): 191–210.
de Baecque, Antoine. 2006. "Le corps au cinéma." In *Histoire du corps: Les mutations du regard. Le XXe siècle*, edited by Jean-Jacques Courtine, 371–91. Paris: Seuil.
Deleuze, Gilles. 1989. *Cinema 2: The Time-Image Cinema*. Translated by Hugh Tomlinson and Robert Galeta. Minneapolis: University of Minnesota Press.
Dine, Philip. 1994. *Images of the Algerian War: French Fiction and Film, 1954–1992*. Oxford: Oxford University Press.
Doane, Mary Ann. 2003. "The Close-up: Scale and Detail in the Cinema." *Differences* 14 (3): 89–111.
Douchet, Jean. 1999. *French New Wave*. Translated by Robert Bunonno. New York: D.A.P.
Feldman, Hannah. 2014. *From a Nation Torn: Decolonizing Art and Representation in France, 1945–1962*. Durham: Duke University Press.
Greene, Naomi. 1999. *Landscapes of Loss: The National Past in Postwar French Cinema*. Princeton: Princeton University Press.
Hayward, Susan. 2005. *French National Cinema* (Second Edition). Abingdon: Routledge.
Higgins, Lynn A. 1996. *New Novel, New Wave, New Politics: Fiction and the Representation of History in Postwar France*. Lincoln and London: University of Nebraska Press.
Ince, Kate. 2017. *The Body and the Screen: Female Subjectivities in Contemporary Women's Cinema*. New York and London: Bloomsbury.
Loshitzky, Yosefa. 1995. *The Radical Faces of Godard and Bertolucci*. Detroit: Wayne State University Press.
Marie, Michel. 2003. *The French New Wave: An Artistic School*. Translated by Richard Neupert. Oxford: Wiley-Blackwell.
Moore, Alison. 2005. "History, Memory, and Trauma in Photography of the *Tondues*: Visuality of the Vichy Past through the Silent Image of Women." *Gender and History* 17 (3): 657–681.
Morrey, Douglas. 2005. *Jean-Luc Godard*. Manchester: Manchester University Press.
Mulvey, Laura and Colin MacCabe. 1980. "Images of Women, Images of Sexuality." In Colin MacCabe, *Godard: Images, Sounds, Politics*, 79–104. London: The MacMillan Press.
Neale, Steve. 1981. "Art Cinema as Institution." *Screen* 22 (1): 11–40.
Neupert, Richard. 2007. *A History of the French New Wave Cinema* (Second Edition). Madison: University of Wisconsin Press.
Nowell-Smith, Geoffrey. 2008. *Making Waves: New Wave, Neorealism, and the New Cinemas of the 1960s*. New York and London: Continuum.
Ross, Kristin. 1996. *Fast Cars, Clean Bodies: Decolonization and the Reordering of French Culture*. Cambridge, MA: The MIT Press.
Schmid, Marion. 2019. *Intermedial Dialogues: The French New Wave and the Other Arts*. Edinburgh: Edinburgh University Press.
Schoonover, Karl. 2012. *Brutal Vision: The Neorealist Body in Postwar Italian Cinema*. Minneapolis: University of Minnesota Press.
Sellier, Geneviève. 2008. *Masculine Singular: French New Wave Cinema*. Translated by Kristin Ross. Durham: Duke University Press.

Sharpe, Mani. 2017. "Screening Decolonisation through Privatisation in Two New Wave Films: *Adieu Philippine* and *La Belle Vie*." *Studies in French Cinema* 17 (2): 129–143.
Vincendeau, Ginette. 2008. "*La Pointe Courte*: How Agnès Varda 'invented' the New Wave." *The Criterion Collection* <https://www.criterion.com/current/posts/497-la-pointe-courte-how-agn-s-varda-invented-the-new-wave>
Vincendeau, Ginette. 2000. *Stars and Stardom in French Cinema*. London: Continuum.

3 Lingering in the men's room

The bathroom, and its attendant spaces—the shower, tub, sink, toilet—is a private space and, as such, almost antithetical to the public displays of cinema. The bathroom is perhaps the place where we are most ourselves, whereas cinema allows us to become someone else. It is where we edit our bodies for public consumption. It is a space of bodily excess and detail, and in this way shares more with cinema than we may readily recognise. The bathroom is largely about secretions, after all, a notion gracefully examined in *Inside Rooms: 26 Bathrooms, London and Oxfordshire* (1985) by Peter Greenaway, whose agenda was wholly verbal:

> It was to be about washing, bathing and batheing, showering, soaking, drying, cleaning, masturbating, playing with rubber ducks, reading damp books, cutting toenails, brushing teeth, gargling, singing to enjoy the echo, expectoration, some copulation, though not so much (too many hard surfaces), considerable looking in mirrors, picking spots, trying to see a good view of your own backside, some vomiting (voluntary and involuntary), and of course urinating and defecating. Urinating and defecating, peeing and shitting, micturating and general elimination. Bodily fluids, as you might expect, were strong on the agenda. Which maybe is as it should be—why not? Bodily fluids make the body go round.
> (Greenaway 2009, 227)

The cinematic bathroom thus gives access to a private world to which one is not *de facto* privy; its public displays outstrip the bathroom's privacy. Since the flushes of its first, then, in Alfred Hitchcock's *Psycho* (1960), fundamentally, all cinematic toilets are public toilets.[1] Indeed, there is a rich yet narrow visual and affective imaginary attached to the cinematic bathroom that has little to do with hygiene and is perhaps best immortalised by an enbubbled Jayne Mansfield in her heart-shaped tub—all male gaze and shag carpets—and lampooned by the relentlessness of Cindy Sherman in her *Untitled Film Stills* (#2 and #81) (Penner 2013). Susan Bordo, however, complicates this imaginary somewhat when she recalls the visceral response she and her

DOI: 10.4324/9781003276241-3

sister had to the centring of Meryl Streep's desire in *The Bridges of Madison County* (Clint Eastwood 1995). Their breathy affect—a gasp—is prompted by a bathroom encounter between the film's lovers: 'in the bathtub, she is transfixed by the drops of water coming from the showerhead that has just recently poured onto his body' (1999, 143). Such is the strength of this deferred contact that it becomes something of a primal scene for Bordo: 'My body was visited by memories of *that* moment in my own life—that moment when a gesture [...] makes what's going to happen clear and unalterable' (143–4; original emphasis). Sealing the unalterable by a simple gesture, this scene likewise secretes the gendered spatiality of the bathroom where femininity equals horizontality and masculinity equals verticality (see Penner 2013, 168; Eleb 2010).

The imaginary inexorably leads to ideology, for whilst accommodating the body's softness—its backside, zits, vomit, shit—the bathroom tacitly confronts this same softness with the hardness 'of pipes and plants' (Penner 2013, 14) and the alternative, less viscous softness 'of social attitudes and beliefs'. Often, soft and hard textures conflate. Soft underconsumption was stimulated by the othering of hard paint colours: *Rose du Barry*, *Orchid of Vincennes* and *Ivoire de Medici* (174). The hard, open design of Anglo-American bathrooms was thought to threaten the softness of (French) femininity (168). The hard (French) bidet threatened a loose (soft) sexuality (182). The litany of hard canvases depicting Turkish baths produced soft orientalist fantasies which ultimately hardened into a Eurocentric imaginary (166–7). Even the humble flush plunges us into the depths of unchecked hegemonic disciplining (14). It is not only water and effluent, then, that pass through the bathroom, and the French bathroom found itself subjected to an Anglo invasion, with layout, flush and toilet paper all US/UK imports (Eleb 2010), an invasion arguably inherited by cinema.

In terms which could easily be applied to film, Robyn Longhurst (2001, 66) suggestively describes bathrooms 'as spaces in which bodily boundaries are broken and then made solid again. They are spaces in which bodies are (re)made and (re)sealed ready for public scrutiny'. Following Christian Metz's seminal intervention on the fundamental fissures that make up the apparatus—cinema/film, discourse/story, institution/text—cinema could hardly be thought of other than as a space for the remaking and resealing of bodies for later public scrutiny: 'The film knows it is being watched, and yet does not know' (1982, 95). This is a seeing and knowing that centres on the presence and absence of bodies in space, and which binds cinema to 'those illicit activities (of exhibitionism and voyeurism) associated with public toilets' (Lyndenberg 2009, 155), as well as to the (typical) solitude of the cubicle and the fetishisms of the keyhole (Metz 1982, 95). Each is thus, as Ruth Barcan notes with reference to the bathroom, 'a physical-psychical space' (2005, 11) or, as Longhurst describes, a site/sight (2001, 66). These considerations are not contemporary inventions; as Georges Vigarello (2005, 315–16) details, the arrival of a systematised water management system in Paris towards the end of the nineteenth century recoded the metropolitan imaginary. The city became a hungry, orificial animal, whilst the bathroom's arrival in the home precipitated both a moral panic and the formation of the private individual by means of the 'me time' it etched out through interdiction: of others, of pleasure, even of nudity (Eleb 2010).

Both bathroom and cinema are, moreover, successful technologies of separation, and whilst Barcan stakes a claim for public toilets as 'the "most culturally visible form" of sexual spatial segregation' (2005, 8), cinema's signage undoubtedly upholds 'the absolute categories of sexual difference' (Lyndenberg 2009, 154)—perhaps coming in a close second. Indeed, France, specifically Paris, is perhaps the birthplace of what Jacques Lacan recorded as 'the laws of urinary segregation' (1977 [1966], 151):

> Perhaps the first mention in history of "Ladies" and "Gentlemen" in this connection is in the report of a great Ball in Paris in 1739, which tells, as of a remarkable innovation, that they had even taken the precaution of allotting *cabinets* with inscriptions over the doors, *Garderobes pour les femmes* and *Garderobes pour les hommes*, with chambermaids in the former and valets in the latter.
>
> (Wright 1960, 103)

However, whether public or private, a distinction to which cinematic bathrooms are, of course, indifferent, the bathroom serves as a technology of gender, for even at home these distinctions prevail, with early twentieth-century bathrooms central to 'an evolution in the role of women and the feminine ideal amongst the bourgeoisie, which dictated the duty of representation but also the necessity of modesty' (Eleb 2010; my translation). This space had a clearly defined *mise en scène*: two vanities, a chimney, a window, a chaise longue and, although private, nothing must betray the 'intimate activities that take place there'. Jugs, buckets, dressing gowns and toiletries must all be kept off stage. Over a century since the advice of la Baronne Staffe was published, such gendering of even the domestic dunny endures. Indeed, as Jennifer Proctor's *Nothing a Little Soap and Water Can't Fix* (2017) makes abundantly clear, within the cinematic vernacular the bathroom site/sight possesses its own distinctive narrative arc, iconography and soundscape: relaxing soakings followed by grisly endings; toes palpating plugholes; anonymous, disembodied hands clasping doors; hinges creaking. There is thus a whole bloody microcinema attached to the on-screen bathroom that dovetails a micropolitics of misogynistic representation. If bodily matter produces cinema, and bodily fluids make the body go round, then it is the brutalised, suffering, imperiled, injured and bleeding bodies of women that produce the cinematic bathroom. Indeed, despite its best efforts, the (public) toilet is a socially polluting space, threatening distinctions of class, gender and sexuality, and threatening what

Mary Douglas (2002 [1966]) diagnoses as the dirt of cultural disorder. If all cinematic toilets are public toilets, they are likely the dirtiest loos too. Simply lingering in the 'restricted space' (Pheasant-Kelly 2006, 201–2) of the bathroom is enough to feminise a body through both (historical) association and its suppression of 'virilising activity', and thus render it vulnerable, at risk. Proctor's cinematic sites/sights might thus be the logical conclusion of these anxious discourses (see also Longhurst [2001]; Pheasant-Kelly [2006]; Eleb [2010]).

French cinema is no exception, for it shares a peculiar history with the bathroom. Coded as part of the 'women's arena' (Betz 2009, 120) within the much-maligned Tradition of Quality, the bathroom bears the promise of feminine undress. It also shares more with the French New Wave than we might initially recognise, regarding questions of privacy and what Geneviève Sellier describes as the 'privatization of representations' (2008, 106), that is, the foregrounding of directorial autobiographical details that have driven French New Wave scholarship and stifled discussions of representation (68–9). For a movement ostensibly unconcerned with psychology, alter egos and ideal egos made in the directors' (bathroom?) mirror image abound. These characters are, as Michel Marie describes with reference to Godard, 'a sort of mouthpiece for the director' (2003, 106). In other words, they are all orifice—a cavity which, Frances Pheasant-Kelly suggests, is 'unequivocally related to' (2006, 196) the bathroom—and these orifical tendencies seep into the industry, for instance, during Agnès Varda's *Palme d'honneur* ceremony in 2015. *Cléo de 5 à 7* was a centrepiece of the celebration, and despite the film's significance to women's filmmaking, as Rebecca DeRoo reflects, the festival screened

> a moment of Cléo's objectification, without hinting at the character's, or the film's, feminist trajectory. In fact, the selection of the sequence at Cannes reinforces gendered notions of creativity often associated with the New Wave [whereby] the audacity of masculine New Wave directors was often associated with the depiction of "modern," scandalously sexual and objectified representations of female characters that were seen to challenge normative roles for women as wives and mothers. Yet Cannes selected a sequence that seems to naturalize this gender dynamic of the movement without overtly acknowledging it. [...] The selection of the Cléo sequence at the festival rehearses often unacknowledged notions of the New Wave and Cannes' priorities.
>
> (2017, 5)

If all cinematic toilets are public toilets, then the French New Wave is a men's room *par excellence*.

Under the tyranny of the first-person masculine singular, this privatisation constitutes a further curiosity and a pseudo-vocality. It reifies the inscription of a determining authorial presence and fosters a fruitful pivot towards the work of Kaja Silverman and Mary Ann Doane on the representation of the profilmic female figure. Whilst such privatisation upholds representation as the preserve of masculinity, the neglect of meaningful, non-libidinal representational innovation exposes the precarity of such masculine privilege (see Doane 1991). In other words, too much is at stake for formal and representational experimentation to take place simultaneously (see Sellier 2008, 77). Is this, then, the Deleuzian prepositional proposition? But *since* the New Wave, every time there has been a fine and powerful film, there has also been a new exploration of the body in it. It is at this juncture that Silverman and Doane can be heard. Theirs is a harmonised project that centres on patriarchal syntagms that structure classical Hollywood representations of women. The bathroom here functions as an exemplary site. A recessed space buried deep within the narrative, its gendered architectonics attest to the triple interiority—diegetic, psychic and corporeal—that yokes women onscreen (Silverman 1988, 70). Indeed, its promise of feminine undress literalises the proprietorial striptease of patriarchy whose ultimate operation aspires to naturalise women's 'discursive lack' (Doane 1991, 167), visually and acoustically (Silverman 1988, 70). As Silverman describes, such 'unveiling' (69)

> follows both from the subordination of the female voice to the female body, and from the enclosure of that voice within narrative recesses and closets. This discursive divestiture works by aligning woman with diegetic interiority, and so by isolating her definitively from the site of textual production.

Such 'diegetic containment' (45) condemns representations of women to spectacle. 'Woman' is always being seen, being heard—caught unawares at the keyhole and condemned to textuality, and resonantly it is the orography of the face in close-up that, for Michel Chion at least, articulates this interiority (Doane 1991, 165). The disclosure of the lip laced with tics like a theatre curtain, the mouth like a ripe fruit splitting open, the keyboard-like smile, all vocal loci, fold women into the diegesis. Yet even her denunciation is a lure for 'the greatest masquerade of all is that of women speaking (or writing, or filming), appropriating discourse' (172). As Doane recognises, however, we do speak, but how this speech occurs may not be clear. Somewhat ironically, the opacity of the body, its insensitivity to or disruption of authorial schemas and/or dominant cinematic structures, offers an exciting site/sight for such impossible speech (Osterweil 2014, 11), and my examination of it here allies this book's aims with a rich field of developing research on cinematic, painterly and photographic representations of women that reimagine corporeality, agency, ideology and horizontality. Across this work, the body precipitates as ideologically resistant and aesthetically innovative (Osterweil 2014, 15; Beugnet 2006, 30), as playfully yet robustly agentic (Ince 2014; Wilson 2019), as appropriative and disruptive (Beugnet 2006, 28; Wilson 2019) and as a conduit for representational justice and kinship (Wilson 2019, 47 and 57). The opacity of women's bodies in Godard's New Wave period channels such qualities and in so doing flushes away the movement's ideology of auteurism and (at times) notorious androcentrism (Sellier 2008, 221–2). Consequently, the female body undoes and reworks the male subjectivity embedded in the films' narratives, at times displacing the male auteur, and his on-screen surrogate, altogether, and it is thus women's bodies, their bodily matter, that produces cinema. This is my contention throughout this book: that despite the authorial displays observable within the films under discussion, and the typical gender dynamic most often observed in French New Wave films, here it is the resistive opacity of women's bodies, their bodily matter, that produces cinema. The body here is verb. It does things to the profilmic.[2]

These principles converge across a quartet of Godard's New Wave films and bathrooms: *À bout de souffle* (1960), *Une femme est une femme* (1961), *Le Mépris* (1963) and *Alphaville* (1965). Bathroom use in *À bout de souffle*, for example, is excessive. Indeed, it structures the film's longest sequence in which Michel and Patricia make three trips together. There are three trips in all in *Une femme est une femme* too, and the bathroom in *Le Mépris* structures another characteristically lengthy domestic sequence (Morrey 2005, 10). Both Camille and Paul take a bath, and soon after having done so, they separate. Finally, bathrooms in *Alphaville* help to take down totalitarianism. In this quartet, Godard's private presence is pervasive, almost excessive—a pervasiveness palpable in the detail. He's there as Michel Poiccard in *À bout de souffle*; he's there via Anna Karina, his wife-muse, in *Une femme est une femme* and *Alphaville*; and his hat, at least, is there in *Le Mépris*, as Paul takes a bath in a trilby. In one sense, the bathroom in each of these films—and the films writ large—operates as Godard's *boudoir*, a place for the passions and messiness of his professional and private lives, which have the tendency to merge. The bathroom, then, is integral to some of the well-documented excesses, and idiosyncrasies, of Godard's film style, and such excesses and idiosyncrasies are obliquely highlighted by Paul B. Franklin in his exploration of the 'queer resonance' (2000, 26) of Marcel Duchamp's *Fountain* (1917). His opening gambit reads:

> Comfort stations, bathrooms, water-closets, urinals, lavatories, toilets, rest rooms, loos, *pissoirs, pissotières, toilettes, petits coins, lieux, vespasiennes, édicules, cabinets d'aisances, chalets de nécessité* ... and the list goes on. The sheer number of English and French terms invented to describe the public spaces into which individuals enter in order to shit and piss reveal a cultural fascination with these base and basic bodily functions.
>
> (25)

Such linguistic plurality indicates a certain national tendency, and readiness, shared by their cross-Channel neighbours to talk about going to the toilet, as well as, following Neale, inadvertently casting the bathroom and its frequent portrayal in (Godard's) French New Wave films as an additional mark of the domestic affiliations that inscribe and (re)construct French national identity. Indeed, its recurrence across Godard's New Wave period parallels, and perhaps even outstrips, the evolving commentary on France's Americanisation, including the souring of relations with this strain of imported modernity, that the car connotes. 'In the early *Breathless* [cars] represented a Beat-style dream of liberation via speed, flexibility, elusiveness' (Sterritt 1999, 97) with toilets, reflecting a comparable freewheeling generic play where a victim of petty thief Michel Poiccard is dispensed with a karate chop (Andrew 1988, 13). However, by the time of *Week-end* (1967), and its infamous escape-to-the-country/journey-to-the-end-of-the-world long take, 'weekend traffic [becomes] today's battlefield [...]. Cars and corpses pile upon the road as a blood offering to the god of highways' (Silverman and Farocki 1998, 83). Across his New Wave films, the *salle de bain* experiences a similar metaphorical decline. For instance, a bathroom, which '70% of the French don't have', features amongst the enigmatic excoriations in the trailer for *Deux ou trois choses que je sais d'elle* (1967)—is the bathroom the 'elle' to which the film's title refers?—whilst its diegetic appearances in this film highlight the pitfalls of modern conveniences when in one scene a meter reading disrupts a young woman's bath, and another scene hammily sends up the invasion of American material culture into contemporary French living (Figure 3.1). Here everything necessary to the usual toilette is present—sink, towels, shower, toothpaste, toothbrush, dressing gown, running water, mirror—yet secreted amongst this iconography are the red and white stripes of the American flag. Invasion is accented further by the 'American' client, who dons a white T-shirt emblazoned with the Stars and Stripes, and his discussion of the ongoing Vietnam War. In this way, Godard's New Wave bathrooms depolarise Lawrence Wright's proposition 'that more [is] to be learned about past

Figure 3.1 An unwelcome meter reading in *Deux ou trois choses que je sais d'elle* (1967).

peoples from their bathrooms than from their battlefields' (1960, x). Instead, the bathroom becomes the battlefield where much is to be learned about past peoples. The lengthy bathroom sequence in *Masculin féminin* (1966) is one such battlefield and exemplifies one of the (sexist) excesses of Godard's film style: the interview. According to Yosefa Loshitzky, 'perhaps more so than any of Godard's other reflexive devices, [the interview] expresses the power relationship between women and men' (1995, 167). Here Paul (Jean-Pierre Léaud) wishes to secure a date with Madeleine (Chantal Goya), but this is no meet cute and instead the pair fiercely interrogate each other about lying, Paul's nose, the meaning of life and sex, which loans the sequence distinctly sociological contours and constitutes an emphatic break with 'the romanticization of the couple and heterosexual love' (143) that permeates the early period of Godard's early period. Thus, the bathroom tracks the shifts in Godard's film style and attitudes.

In the bathroom, Madeleine preens, brushing her hair and applying lipstick, and Paul smokes, vapour escaping from his mouth and nose. Madeleine scoffs, Paul attempts a compliment and, through such derision, failure, and everyday acts, the body bodies forth in ways that figure as decidedly Godardian, for example, through discourse (enumeration, conversation, blazon), rather than intercourse, and decidedly un-Godardian. For through a series of involuntary movements, the camera reveals what lies beneath the skin—lungs, muscles, ligaments—and what escapes authorial control and resists conjugation in the masculine singular. The body's base, inherent amateurishness cannot help but admit access to the real, and what Béla Balázs 'considered […] guarantors of authenticity capable of revealing "the hidden life of little things"' (Osterweil 2014, 201). Nana's gulps, and perhaps her blinking and lip licking, in the opening triptych of *Vivre sa vie* (1962), which is famed for its overwhelmingly controlled portraiture, are similar guarantors and counter Godard's control, whilst François Truffaut tries to tame Léaud's gauche artlessness in *Baisers volés* (1968).

Whether *boudoir*, battlefield or Balázsian, the bathroom gives us a further privileged site/sight for thinking about New Wave bodies, and, moreover, it is at the very level of the 'interpenetration of life and cinema' (Morrey 2005, 25) that we might start to restore these bodies to film criticism. Interpenetrating, life and cinema form the same folds and frictions as the embracing, striking, intertwining, bumping bodies that Gilles Deleuze locates within French New Wave films. Their nestling is verbal, it does things to the profilmic, and onscreen bodies constitute a fundamental part of this 'vanishing point' of representational (re)productions, as Douglas Morrey identifies in his sweeping appraisal of Godard's cinema. He writes:

> The paradox is, if anything, all the stranger in cinema which composes with *real* bodies, *real* objects and *real* light: the film image is that obscure point of convergence where fantasy becomes reality and reality fantasy,

where the unconscious desire of both filmmakers and spectators achieve a fleshy incarnation just as the recorded reality recedes behind a fictional representation.

(Original emphasis)

Morrey's words could be read as a description of the bathroom with its promise of unconscious desire becoming fleshy incarnation, where reality and fantasy intermingle. They also cast the body as verbal; its realness does something to the profilmic, confusing the contours between fantasy and reality. Bodily matter thus produces cinema, signalling its realist credentials, while constructing its phantasmal ones. Whether *boudoir*, battlefield or Balázsian, whether realist or phantasmal, the bathroom ensures that we do not lose sight of the actual body, and it is to Godard's New Wave bodies, and their occupation of perhaps cinema's ultimate men's room, and *salles de bain*, that we now turn.

Notes

1 For Ara Osterweil (2014), the film's shower scene 'displace[s] the ejaculatory vulnerability of the male subject onto a woman' (181) and emblematises how 'the sadism of Hollywood's male gaze comes in the form of the cut, which assimilates the splice of celluloid to the incision of female flesh' (207). Godard achieves a parallel effect via a graphic match cut in *Le Petit Soldat* (1960), which sees Bruno hop from the living room to the bathroom as he pulls on his jumper.
2 A perverse urtext for such discussion could be Louis Malle's *Viva Maria!* (1965) and its tale of revolution, synchronization and striptease.

References

Andrew, Dudley. 1988. *Breathless: Jean-Luc Godard, Director*. New Brunswick: Rutgers University Press.

Barcan, Ruth. 2005. "Dirty Spaces: Communication and Contamination in Men's Public Toilets." *Journal of International Women's Studies* 6 (2): 7–23.

Beugnet, Martine. 2006. "Close-up vision: Re-mapping the body in the work of contemporary French women filmmakers." *Nottingham French Studies* 45 (3): 24–38.

Bordo, Susan. 1999. *The Male Body: A New Look at Men in Public and in Private*. New York: Farrar, Straus and Giroux.

DeRoo, Rebecca J. 2017. *Agnès Varda Between Film, Photography, and Art*. Oakland: University of California Press.

Doane, Mary Ann. 1991. *Femmes Fatales: Feminism, Film Theory and Psychoanalysis*. London: Routledge.

Douglas, Mary. 2002 [1966]. *Purity and Danger: An Analysis of Concept of Pollution and Taboo*. London: Routledge.

Eleb, Monique. 2010. "La mise au propre en architecture." *Techniques & Culture* 54–55: 558–609.

Franklin, Paul B. 2000. "Object Choice: Marcel Duchamp's Fountain and the Art of Queer Art History." *Oxford Art Journal* 23 (1): 23–50.

Greenaway, Peter. 2009. "Afterword." In *Ladies and Gents: Public Toilets and Gender*, edited by Olga Gershenson and Barbara Penner, 227–30. Philadelphia: Temple University Press.

Ince, Kate. 2017. *The Body and the Screen: Female Subjectivities in Contemporary Women's Cinema*. New York and London: Bloomsbury.

Lacan, Jacques. 1977 [1966]. *Écrits: A Selection*. Translated by Alan Sheridan. London: Tavistock Publications.

Longhurst, Robyn. 2001. *Bodies: Exploring Fluid Boundaries*. London: Routledge.

Loshitzky, Yosefa. 1995. *The Radical Faces of Godard and Bertolucci*. Detroit: Wayne State University Press.

Metz, Christian. 1982. *Psychoanalysis and Cinema: The Imaginary Signifier*. Translated by Celia Britton, Annwyl Williams, Ben Brewster and Alfred Guzzetti. London: The Macmillan Press.

Morrey, Douglas. 2005. *Jean-Luc Godard*. Manchester: Manchester University Press.

Osterweil, Ara. 2014. *Flesh Cinema: The Corporeal Turn in American Avant-garde Film*. Manchester: Manchester University Press.

Penner, Barbara. 2013. *Bathroom*. London: Reaktion Books.

Pheasant-Kelly, Frances. 2009. "In the Men's Room: Death and Derision in Cinematic Toilets." In *Ladies and Gents: Public Toilets and Gender*, edited by Olga Gershenson and Barbara Penner, 195–207. Philadelphia: Temple University Press.

Sellier, Geneviève. 2008. *Masculine Singular: French New Wave Cinema*. Translated by Kristin Ross. Durham: Duke University Press.

Silverman, Kaja. 1988. *The Acoustic Mirror: The Female Voice in Psychoanalysis and Cinema*. Bloomington: Indiana University Press.

Silverman, Kaja and Harun Farocki. 1998. *Speaking about Godard*. New York: New York University Press.

Sterritt, David. 1999. *The Films of Jean-Luc Godard: Seeing the Invisible*. Cambridge: Cambridge University Press.

Vigarello, Georges. 2005. "Hygiène du corps et travail des apparences." In *Histoire du corps: De la Révolution à la Grande Guerre*, edited by Alain Corbin, 307–20. Paris: Seuil.

Wilson, Emma. 2019. *The Reclining Nude: Agnès Varda, Catherine Breillat, and Nan Goldin*. Liverpool: Liverpool University Press.

Wright, Lawrence. 1960. *Clean and Decent: The Fascinating History of the Bathroom & the Water Closet and of Sundry Habits, Fashions & Accessories of the Toilet Principally in Great Britain, France, & America*. New York: The Viking Press.

4 Of aliens and alter egos

Pa-Pa-Pa-Patricia, sings Jean-Paul Belmondo's plosive petty thief and soon-to-be cop killer, Michel Poiccard, *en route* to *Pa-Pa-Pa-Paris* in a stolen Alpha Romeo in Jean-Luc Godard's New Wave debut, *À bout de souffle* (1960). Like all opportunistic shower cubicle crooners, Poiccard clearly 'enjoy[s] the sound of his own voice' (Morrey 1995, 9), and his singing to enjoy the echo briefly transforms his ride into an ersatz bathroom and anticipates the trio of comfort stations that feature in Godard's first contribution to the desanitising efforts of the French New Wave. Facilitating film *noir*-inspired robberies and getaways, as well as the usual salubrious suspects, such as urinating and washing, public conveniences and private privies are taken over by the same imitative economy that shapes *À bout de souffle*'s authorship, characters, iconography and style, and scores its critical reception.[1]

One such reading locates this imitation in the bathroom. Examining how the film enacts the Lacanian mirror stage through both its emulation of Hollywood cinema and the lead protagonist's emulation of one of its stars, Humphrey Bogart, Dennis Turner deploys the bathroom mirror as a site for the dangers of this psychical phenomenon, commenting how Michel and Patricia's relationship to this specular surface, and by extension the space of the bathroom, exposes and derails 'narcissistic identification with the projected self' (1983, 60). Turner identifies this dynamic in one of the most discussed sequences of Godard's oeuvre: Michel's visit to Patricia in room 14 of the Hotel de Suède, where despite the restricted space available to them, their bodies are very active. Indeed, this restriction encourages their proximity. Slapping, kissing, clambering, brushing, leaning, smoking, caressing, bending, grimacing, mimicking, making love, the body here is verb. When in the bathroom, however, as Turner notes, bodies are resolute objects of fascination for the pair. Both are drawn to the mirror: they like to watch their bodies at work, doing bodywork—brushing hair and eyebrows, washing faces and feet, applying scent—as if searching for the realness of their bodies through this labour (Figure 4.1). Their recurrent visits to this room suggest a continued search. Theirs is a flesh that continually seeks to recede behind fictional representations: Humphrey Bogart, an alien, a soldier, even each other when

DOI: 10.4324/9781003276241-4

Figure 4.1 Poiccard (Jean-Paul Belmondo) and Patricia (Jean Seberg) doing bodywork in the bathroom.

they don complementary stripes. Their continued masquerade traps Poiccard and Patricia on a carousel; round and round they go, held in place by 'their sadly circumscribed vocabularies' (Sterritt 1999, 60), 'trapped in [a] logic of citation' (Morrey 2005, 26), which programmes costumes, behaviours, final words and the film's denouement (Kline 1992, 199–200). Not even death admits respite from this false carnival. The opacity of the body, however, does—and, as this chapter will explore, the body corrodes authorial, personal expression and counterpoints the restrictive circuits of meaning that the film's reverential trappings of genre realise.

This corrosive, contrapuntal corporeality is delicately established in the Hotel de Suède sequence, in which, despite her numerous costume changes, Patricia's visits to the bathroom do not bear the promise of feminine undress. In an example of cross-undressing, this promise lies with Michel, for throughout the sequence Poiccard's bare torso and limbs hyperbolically inscribe him into the space. The excesses of his epidermis produce something of an obscenity, which through its exorbitant visuality makes manifest the contingencies of the flesh: a scar at the mouth and the nose, a tuft of hair at the clavicle. His body dominates this scene, during which the trappings of genre fall away.[2] It thus constitutes cinematic excess. Moreover, it lingers, taking up nearly a third of the film's runtime. Poiccard's semi-nudity assiduously reflects such 'narrative stasis' (Fotiade 2013, 75). His undress disrupts the film's generic promise and narrows the gap between fantasy and reality. He can no longer hide behind the bluster of the film's/Godard's 'postmodern bravado' (69). He is literally stripped of 'the unambiguous pastiche of the American gangster-movie dress code: the elegant suit, the hat, the dark glasses' (75), although the striptease takes place off-screen, arguably diminishing any (initial) risk of divestiture.

Michel Marie is equally sensitive to questions of dress here, and his analysis aligns clothing and corporeality. 'The representation of the body', he writes, 'takes place [...] through undressing' (92; my translation), while his account is equally attuned to the choreography of 'bodies'.

> The camera does not stop tracking the actors' movements, detailing all their gestures. Patricia's thumb removing ash from Michel's face. Patricia counting on her fingers when Michel asks if she regularly slept with boys in New York. Michel caressing her knee, straightening her chin with his fingertips.
>
> (91–2)

'It is through these prosaic details' (92), he continues, 'that the body is *mise en scène*'. In part, Marie here hints at the primacy of the body, gesturing to the frictions, collisions and caresses, the proximity through which French New Wave bodies create worlds and animate major sequences with the delicate and dexterous work of hands notably foregrounded. Yet, prepositionally speaking, Marie's account deputises the body. It is only because of these other offerings that the body is represented. Poiccard's exposed epidermis seemingly composes the antidote to this, its sense of autonomy subtly affirmed as Patricia regards Michel through a rolled-up Renoir. Her/the camera's gaze homes in on Poiccard like an iris out—a shot Godard intermittently pastiches throughout the film—and through such orifical framing, the film tries to scaffold what turns out to be an ill-fitting aesthetic onto Belmondo's body. During an earlier mirror moment, Godard has similar recourse to this 'antiquated device' (1983, 56), which Turner understands as both a pull towards textuality and a sign of authorial control, teasing his body from the privacy of the diegesis, surrendering it to the public of enunciation. It imprisons Poiccard, pointing up the textual net in which he unknowingly finds himself caught. The film knows, though, its omniscience rendering Michel curiously vulnerable, according to classic cinematic vernacular where male characters are routinely aligned with 'discursive authority' (Silverman 1988, 21), safely (yet illusorily) placed on the side of enunciation. Any attempt to confine Michel is, however, usurped by a two shot of the most intimate nature: an embrace that the scene twice takes to epidermal extremes.

Hyperbolic, monstrous, gigantic, organic: in the first instance, their faces are presented as a single fleshy landscape, a corporeal chiasm, which slowly

32 Of aliens and alter egos

Figure 4.2 Au biseau des baisers/Kisses on the edge.

precipitates through a series of identifiable facial markers (eyebrows, eyelashes, sideburns, stubble, lips, wrinkles, ears, hairlines) and orifices (sockets, nostrils, mouths, concha), intimating an intimacy with the bathroom along with the authorial mouthpiece. Kissing, the body spills out as a non-verbalised catalogue of parts; it prompts a further narrative stall through its indulgence in excess and detail and does not require an elaborate choreography to be *mise en scène*. The face is not treated as a ledger of subjectivity, that is, as a means to better determine his fancy and her whimsy—will she sleep with Michel or not?—but rather as a facet of corporeality, as muscular, as mucous, as hairy: as a facticity, which emerges through the pressure produced by the proximity of their bodies (Figure 4.2).

This shot and pressure is repeated later in the film when Poiccard and Patricia seek refuge in the cinema. Marie-Claire Ropars-Wuilleumier maps these epidermal extremes onto her expansive understanding of montage, or what she calls 'hieroglyphic editing' (1982, 147). With the potential to combine, and divide, all manner of things, such as sound, image, objects, letters, gestures, the hieroglyph, 'causes signification to shatter into heterogenous networks'. In Ropars's account, it is agentic and distributive. Given its ability to mobilise, dissociate and fragment heterogenous elements, cinema is especially well suited to such shattering, scattering or wavering of signification; Ropars calls it a 'vocation' and categorises this latter shot as one of the film's 'privileged fracture zones' where we witness 'the activity of writing, conceived in the hieroglyphic form of editing' at work. Poiccard and Patricia's kiss typifies this hieroglyphic editing through its assembly of sound, image, poetry and, of course, bodies. Whilst the imagetrack depicts their kiss, the soundtrack consists of extracts from poems by Apollinaire and Aragon that evidently cannot be uttered by the film's leads, as 'their lips are busy' (148). The usual coincidence of image- and soundtrack comes apart, its unity broken, whilst 'poetic writing' intrudes into the cinematic and usurps the place of dialogue to set up the medley of associations prized and enabled by hieroglyphic editing. In this way, their kiss marshals, 'in condensed form' (Rodowick 2001, 97), the decidedly lettered, if not exclusively literary, textual system that infiltrates Godard's film. As D. N. Rodowick summarises:

> The circulation of "letters" forms a particularly dense network of association in Ropars's analysis of the film. For example, the line voiced from Aragon in sequence 10 ("Au biseau des baisers") is condensed into a paragrammatic formula (Abdbs) that, according to Ropars, circulates willfully in the film, inscribing itself at one point in a fragment of a movie poster ("Vivre dangeureusement, jusqu'au bout"), in the vocal alliteration of the Aragon poem ("souvenir brisés"), and in the title of a book enlarged on the screen (*Abracadabra*). It thus describes a circuit of traces that ultimately returns to the title of the film: *À bout de souffle*.
>
> (2001, 97)

Agentic and distributive, like the hieroglyph, this paragrammatic formula (Abdbs) and 'density' (Ropars 1982, 152) gets denser still upon the realisation that the French bathroom, the *salle de bain* or sdb, echoes the film's 'errant alphabet'. Consequently, every trip to the *salle de bain* further distributes Ropars's textual system through the film, *jusqu'au bout*, as we will come to see. Equally, it indicates that the similarity between these intimate two shots is far from arbitrary, especially as the first example constitutes a fleshy threshold to Patricia's bathroom.

Ropars also recognises the correspondences between these two shots, considering them oppositional owing to their radically different spatio-temporal configurations. Whereas the bedroom sequence, which houses the first kiss, 'is inscribed in an easily spotted spatio-temporal continuity' (148), their later kiss is ensconced in a 'rift' and adrift from identifiable spatial and temporal markers. Nonetheless, the 'cabalistic' (153) workings of the paragrammatic formula (Abdbs) are legible in the earlier scene because, kissing on the threshold of the bathroom/*salle de bain*, Poiccard and Patricia's bodies not only neighbour but recombine the original formula. *Au biseau des baisers*, Abdbs, on the edge of kisses, becomes kisses on the edge, or *des baisers au biseau*, dbsab. Whilst in Ropars's account, cinema sublimates the book (148), the film's paragrammatic formula amplifies the role of bodies in the original heterogenous admixture of the hieroglyph. Here, bodies do not simply comprise a projection screen for what intrudes upon the diegesis, but active, shattering components, and they hint that all cinema is potentially on the precipice of collapse into its fundamental heterogeneity—a threat that the close-up bolsters. After all, the uncanny intimacies that the close-up may occasion are a result of the body torn apart, from its surroundings and from 'the body of the *récit*' (Beugnet 2006, 25). Such tears suggest that the close-up is always a hieroglyph in waiting, and here they undermine Ropars's belief in the spatio-temporal coherence of Poiccard and Patricia's first edgy embrace. A quick cut, and a radically new arrangement of bodies, from apart to together, frays its edges and, like Ropars's privileged fracture zones, briefly unmoors Poiccard and Patricia from the familiar surrounds of room 14 of the Hotel de Suède—it is only their corporeality of which we can be certain. Indeed, such hieroglyphic latency propels the film's paragrammatic formula beyond its contours and towards the cinema of Guy Gilles, and his 1959 short set in Algiers about the volatility of young love, *Au biseau des baisers* (co-directed with Marc Sator), which includes a bathtub as part of its opening credit sequence, and the influential work of Benjamin Stora who 'perceived' (Dine 1994, 220) Poiccard 'as the screen representative of that young generation of Frenchmen condemned to serve, suffer and even die in Algeria'. As what T. Jefferson Kline names the film's 'graphic unconscious' (1992, 188), this medley of prized associations surreptitiously, and perhaps compulsively, nudges *À bout de souffle* towards the unsayable: the then-ongoing Algerian War of Independence (1954–62). Although their landing right back in the bathroom reinforces its original paragrammatic formula, it does not necessarily extinguish this relational network given the hygienic imaginary that shapes discussions of the war (see Chapter 7). Like the scene overall, it lingers and confirms the agentic and ideologically resistant qualities of the body, which silently secretes subversion, for these circuits circumvent censorship. Perhaps inadvertently, then, and unlike much New Wave criticism, Ropars's textual system accommodates the body and prepares the critical ground for the sequence's second independently fleshy incarnation, Patricia, through the assault on textual unity her corporeality enacts.

Like many female French New Wave characters, Patricia's body is frequently at risk of being equated with 'mass culture's visual detritus' (Paige 2004, 5). She is often framed alongside reproductions of classic and contemporary masters, perhaps most famously her two shot with Renoir's portrait of Irène Cahen d'Anvers (c. 1880), which takes place in the bathroom. During such moments, she is understood in relation to two-dimensional, sanitised imitation: an imitative corporeal economy whose art-historical pulse upholds New Wave frontality, much like the pair's mutual fascination with the bathroom mirror does. As such, Patricia is tacitly enmeshed in the alienation-consumption corollary that co-opts and industrialises women's bodies by means of a toilette that necessitates painting and sculpting 'a look of femininity, a look which is a guarantee of *visibility* in sexist society for each individual woman' (Mulvey and MacCabe 1980, 90; original emphasis). However, the sequence accords her a less compromised sense of embodiment too. Her shoulders, arms, elbows, knees, wrists, fingertips and nape are all attended to by the camera, and by Poiccard's hands, and alongside these more obvious body parts, more discreet fleshy indices can be spotted: moles, pimples and wispy hairs on her arms and legs that cannot help but catch the light. Real bodies illuminated with real light, the body on-screen always transports something of the amateur that signifies a lack of (authorial) control, the threat of corporeal excess or excrescences. Intriguingly, in these moments of scrutiny, Patricia is often acephalic. Her face is not the locus of eroticism, merely a(n off-screen) carnal appendage. Indeed, it is her knees that prove especially fleshy as Poiccard's/the camera's caresses linger on them, anticipating the titular obsession of Éric Rohmer's *Le genou de Claire* (1970) in which a single body part outstrips the auteur as the primary organising principle, realising a positive move beyond the innovation/representation impasse.

Once again here, through the friction of the caress, bodily matter produces cinema, and by means of a seemingly unambiguous subject-object optic, we might interpret these moments as further instances wherein the on-screen body—here Patricia's—is at risk, this time from Poiccard's desire, masculine desire, and the nestled triptych of looks that comprise the male gaze (see Mulvey 1975). Yet it is in these apparently riskiest moments that Patricia's corporeality is at its most opaque, agentic and ideologically resistant. The knee, after all, brings its own obscenity. It ruins the coveted, idealised seamlessness analysed by Roland Barthes in *Mythologies* (1972 [1952]), and as a joint it 'constitute[s] the obscene of the object-world' (Ross 1996, 147) for it betrays labour, in this case the labour that goes into being a body. It marks the object, and here the body, with the nightmare of (re)production by summoning assembly and the assembly line, which Godard's imaginary museum naturalises. In this way, Patricia's knee acts as saboteur, for it discreetly reproaches the industrialisation of women's bodies (Figure 4.3).

Patricia, of course, is not the only body on the factory floor, and here we glimpse Poiccard's 'dismembered hand' (Silverman 1988, 194) operating as a stand-in for Godard's authorial voice by dictating the shot's cinematography. Following his tactile exploration of Patricia's skin, a look of troubled uncertainty flashes across Poiccard's face. He suspects that something is off but can't quite put his finger on it despite his digital perusal. Whatever the machinations of his mind here, his caress compounds his proxy status because this is a voice, as Kaja Silverman details via Barthes, relegated to scriptor 'borne by a pure gesture of inscription (and not of expression)' that betrays the true labour of textual production: '"writing" designates a way of reading

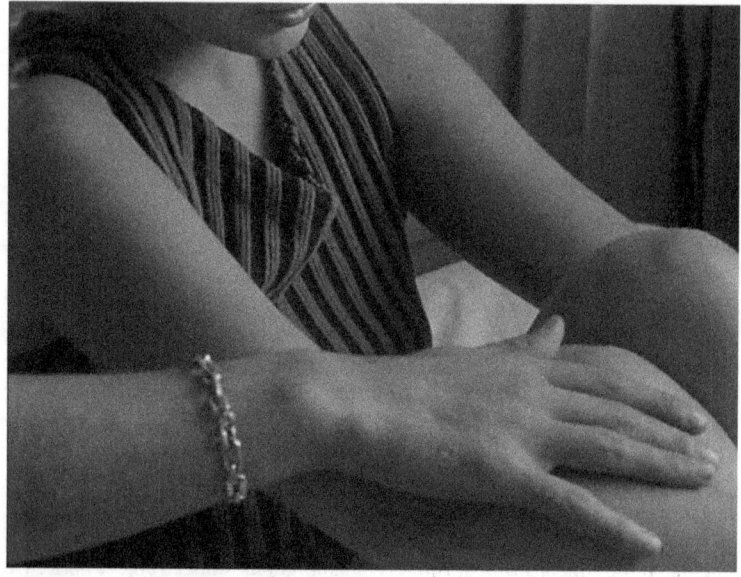

Figure 4.3 Patricia, the acephalic saboteur.

which discloses the cluster or "braid" of quotations that make up a text' (189). Through such writing and reading, as Silverman describes:

> The author is [...] subjected to a double displacement: First, the "voices" of culture replace him as the speaking agency behind the text, and as a consequence unitary meaning gives way to discursive heterogeneity and contestation. Second, because this plurality is activated only through and "in" the reader, he or she supplants the author as the site at which the text comes together.

Thanks to this palimpsestic writing and reading, which resonates with the dual forces of Ropars's hieroglyphic editing, knitting and splintering meaning, Michel Poiccard exists. However, he is not a beneficiary of the polyvalence that this palimpsestic writing and reading permits. In fact, it narrows Poiccard's existential horizon. He is nothing more than a cluster of quotations. Perhaps, then, it is not his tumble into diegetic interiority that Poiccard reads on the (comparatively) blank(er) page of Patricia's skin, but rather a future free from citation that would rewrite his own fate. What would have become of the film, of Poiccard and Patricia, if he had jumped off the programmatic carousel of generic citation and embraced the film's paragrammatic formula and shattering of the hieroglyph, that is, if he had permanently abandoned the postmodern braid that makes up Michel Poiccard? What alternative assemblages of sound, image, objects, letters and gestures could his body have materialised?

The scene's most insistent flirtation with this opportunity occurs when, unusually for a Godardian New Wave couple, discourse slides into intercourse and the pair embark on a Franco-American rapprochement beneath the sheets. For many, their intertwining represents the scene's denouement. Yet these covers also operate as a blank canvas, briefly dematerialising the body and literalising the tabula rasa that would liberate Michel. The scene also attempts another privileged fracture zone, this time with a radio broadcast muscling in on the dialogue. Such speculative fiction, however, is consistently thwarted, and it is Patricia, whom Poiccard entreats to match his state of undress, who neutralises it by putting on more clothes. She dons his trilby and then reads the final line from William Faulkner's *The Wild Palms* (1939) a little too late to form a privileged fracture zone—too much unity—whilst her post-coital mention of Dylan Thomas's *Portrait of the Artist as a Young Dog* (1940) is fleeting at most. She further circulates Michel's tough guy cluster by sporting his shirt before lobbing it at him, whilst her lit cigarettes hang heavier in her mouth as the scene progresses.

Patricia's *mise en scène* thus effortlessly plays with the braid of quotations that makes up Michel Poiccard, and in doing so, she channels the agentic and distributive promise of the hieroglyph, modelling its centripetal and centrifugal forces. By reworking the suspicion, displacement and reproduction that define Godard's incoherent relationship to images of women during much of his New Wave period, Patricia subtly reclaims female agency and effectively casts 'the author as receiver' (Pantenburg 2015, 243), who in turn does nothing more than pick up the signals of the voices that replace him as the speaking agency behind the text. Thanks to such palimpsestic writing and reading, Patricia's knee continues its synovial sabotage and wrests agentic and literary action from the combined clutches of Poiccard/Godard, whose pestering touch becomes an anxious caress that seriously unsettles selfhood. Indeed, he is so overcome by the keen sensation of Patricia's body that he recourses to his Bogey mouth gesture as if to (re)affirm his own (imitative) corporeality, and soon enough, having spent the preceding 15 minutes of the film in white boxer shorts and a striped bathrobe, Michel dresses and regains his delinquent braid. Patricia's body thus supplants the author as the site at which the text comes together, textually producing both Poiccard and Godard through the cascade of generic trappings that return to the film (phone calls to associates, soon-to-be stolen cars, his gangster getup). Thus inscribed, the auteur becomes just another art cinema body. Thus inscribed, Poiccard's/Godard's discursive authority stalls. Startlingly so, as the profilmic female figure is conventionally used to overwrite lack, rather than to expose it.

We also see this anxious caress in action in *Masculin féminin* (1966). Here Jean-Pierre Léaud's Paul increasingly finds himself excluded from the film's sexual economy (Loshitzky 1995, 143), and, appropriately, the bathroom crystallises his marginalisation. In the film, it is a decidedly women-only space, and even in the men's room, Paul finds himself excluded, ignored by the couple whose kiss he interrupts. What's more, his exclusion coincides with the film's textual economy becoming increasingly encroached upon by other New Wave texts and bodies. Cameos from Brigitte Bardot and Antoine Bourseiller in one café scene hyperbolise this trespass, the Swedish art film that the film's core quartet go to see obliquely reveals *Masculin féminin*'s financial intrusions (that is, its status as a co-production), and in Paul's final scene Madeleine and Catherine-Isabelle (Catherine Duport) ridicule any resemblance he may have to Jean-Paul Belmondo, evoked here as a mix of Michel Poiccard's four-wheel thievery and the titular character of *Pierrot le fou* (1965), whilst Paul's mention of 'General Doinel' in the war office recalls Léaud's on-screen debut in François Truffaut's *Les 400 coups* (1959). Paul attempts to combat his marginalisation by means of the caress, intermittently stroking Madeleine's arm or face. These caresses are only ever belatedly acknowledged, if at all, and occasionally mocked, and fundamentally they consolidate his exteriority. The film's denouement seals Paul's expulsion. In something of a Deleuzian gesture, he falls from a window of the 'unfinished apartment' (2001 [1986], 124) he has recently purchased and thereby joins the ranks of French New Wave fetish actors dying on the Parisian pavement.

Michel Poiccard inaugurates this mortal roll call and, before expiring, he performs one of his corporeal tics—*aah, eeh, ooh*—and (apparently) calls Patricia *dégueulasse*. His accusation persists as an enigma as much to Patricia and the policeman as to the cinema-going public and half a century's worth of criticism inspired by the film, complementing the polyvalence that the hieroglyphic and palimpsestic writing and reading championed by this chapter enables.[3] In a gesture that upholds the imitative generic and corporeal cores of the film, Patricia does not reply in kind to Michel. Instead, she reflects his hero back to him like a failed mirror, or like a hieroglyph that gathers the film's infamous gestures, and traces her lips using Poiccard's Bogey hand gesture, before asking, *qu'est-ce que c'est dégueulasse?* Once more, her body, and tellingly her hand, discloses the true labour of textual production: inscription upon inscription upon inscription. Bogey. Poiccard. Bogey. Patricia. As such, Patricia is not a 'treacherous enigma' (Loshitzky 1995, 138) but rather a beacon of full disclosure. Her body is the very basis of the book on the French New Wave body that we might begin—agentic, appropriative, resistant—and, moreover, it marshals other textual bodies. *Qu'est-ce que c'est dégueulasse?* With no answer forthcoming, Patricia turns her back on us, overriding the frontal schema of the French New Wave. *Dégueulasse*, however, continues to hang in the air, and on everyone's lips, and it reconjures the cabalistic workings of the film's paragrammatic formula, drawing them out *jusqu'au bout*, perhaps even solving the stubborn mystery of its final words, *Qu'est-ce que c'est dégueulasse?* Perhaps it is an (un)hygienic hieroglyph that adopts the bathroom's expectorant-relaxant schema, which see-saws, instead of carousels, Poiccard, Patricia and the spectator between expulsion (*dégueuler*) and ennui (*lasse*)—an oscillation for which corporeality is the lynchpin.

Notes

1 See, for instance, Douglas Morrey on the joyful cinephilia the film exhibits (2005, 8); David Sterritt on how the film reflects Godard's 'cultural kleptomania' (1999, 54); and T. Jefferson Kline on the ironic 'simulation' the film enacts through its relationship with classical Hollywood narrative cinema and its later American remake (1992, 184–5).
2 See Michel Marie (1999), p. 91 and Morrey (2005), pp. 10–11. Alternative readings suggest that this scene in fact intensifies the film's generic identity or hybridity. James Tweedie considers it a documentary on youth and rebellion (2013, 107), whilst Dudley Andrew calls it a 'Hollywood love story' (1988, 11).
3 Ironically, disgust works otherwise. It polices. It is something we all need to agree on, or else it is meaningless. It comes apart. See Ahmed (2014).

References

Ahmed, Sara. 2014. *The Cultural Politics of Emotion* (Second Edition). Edinburgh: Edinburgh University Press.
Andrew, Dudley. 1988. *Breathless: Jean-Luc Godard, Director*. New Brunswick: Rutgers University Press.
Barthes, Roland. 1972 [1957]. *Mythologies*. Translated by Annette Lavers. New York: The Noonday Press.
Beugnet, Martine. 2006. "Close-up Vision: Re-mapping the Body in the Work of Contemporary French Women Filmmakers." *Nottingham French Studies* 45 (3): 24–38.
Deleuze, Gilles. 2001 [1986]. *Cinema 1: The Movement Image*. Translated by Hugo Tomlinson and Barbara Habberjam. London: Continuum.
Dine, Philip. 1994. *Images of the Algerian War: French Fiction and Film, 1954–1992*. Oxford: Oxford University Press.
Fotiade, Ramona. 2013. *À bout de souffle*. London: I.B. Tauris.
Kline, T. Jefferson. 1992. *Screening the Text: Intertextuality in French New Wave Cinema*. Baltimore: The Johns Hopkins University Press.
Loshitzky, Yosefa. 1995. *The Radical Faces of Godard and Bertolucci*. Detroit: Wayne State University Press.
Marie, Michel. 1999. *À bout de souffle: Jean-Luc Godard*. Paris: Éditions Nathan.
Morrey, Douglas. 2005. *Jean-Luc Godard*. Manchester: Manchester University Press.
Mulvey, Laura. 1975. "Visual Pleasure and Narrative Cinema." *Screen* 16 (3): 6–18.
Mulvey, Laura and Colin MacCabe. 1980. "Images of Women, Images of Sexuality." In *Godard: Images, Sounds, Politics*, edited by Colin MacCabe, 79–104. London: The MacMillan Press.
Paige, Nicholas. 2004. "Bardot and Godard in 1963 (Historicizing the Postmodern Image)." *Representations* 88 (1): 1–25.
Pantenburg, Volker. 2015. *Farocki/Godard: Film as Theory*. Amsterdam: Amsterdam University Press.

Rodowick, David. 2001. *Reading the Figural, or, Philosophy after the New Media*. Durham: Duke University Press.
Ropars-Wuilleumier, Marie-Claire. 1982. "The Graphic in Filmic Writing: *À bout de souffle*, or the Erratic Alphabet." *Enclitic* 5 (2)/6 (1): 147–61.
Silverman, Kaja. 1988. *The Acoustic Mirror: The Female Voice in Psychoanalysis and Cinema*. Bloomington: Indiana University Press.
Sterritt, David. 1999. *The Films of Jean-Luc Godard: Seeing the Invisible*. Cambridge: Cambridge University Press.
Turner, Dennis. 1983. "Mirror Stage of the Nouvelle Vague." *Substance* 12 (4): 50–63.
Tweedie, James. 2013. *The Age of New Waves: Art Cinema and the Staging of Globalization*. Oxford: Oxford University Press.

5 Of bathroom sinks and the streets below

À bout de souffle (1960) transitions us seamlessly into a discussion of *Une femme est une femme* (1961), for mention of the former film in the latter inaugurates its relationship with the bathroom. Jean-Paul Belmondo, here playing Alfred, best friend of Jean-Claude Brialy's Émile and lover of Anna Karina's Angéla, comments that Godard's debut feature is on television that evening, only to be ushered across the bathroom's threshold moments later. If the author is receiver, here he has apparently worked out a way of reassuringly picking up his own signals. Tucked away in one corner of Angéla and Émile's flat, the bathroom in *Une femme est une femme* is a fickle site, supplying water only with the tap of a hammer, and it is always a site of the failed communication that distinguishes New Wave couples. Nonsense and drivel dribble out in tautology and toothpaste (see also Ezra 2014). The bathroom operates as a curiously autonomous site too, somehow alive within the confines of Angéla and Émile's apartment who exploit the (supposed) privacy that it admits—Angéla sequesters Alfred away upon her first visit to the water closet—as well as its quotidian functionality. During her second and third trips, Angéla brushes her teeth and almost showers. This autonomy is especially palpable in the seemingly sourceless light that beats in the room. Windmilling between a soft, delicate turquoise and an intense, vivid red, this light fills the room, though its lights are out. These enigmatic illuminations hyperbolise the real bodies, objects and light, and elemental heterogeneity, out of which cinema is composed. Books, as we will come to see, are equally imbricated in this hyperbolisation that coincides with the bathroom, such as when Angéla and Alfred tease Émile during the film's first visit to the water closet. In response to his exclusion, Émile inaudibly mutters *merde*, circles the flat on his bike and then resorts to reading a book. In doing so, he inadvertently animates the blue glow that limns the apartment windows and the red of a lampshade in such a way that mirrors the alternating enigmatic lights that fill the bathroom—an effect echoed by Angéla's red cardigan and Émile's blue jacket. This shifting configuration of bodies, books and light thus informs the concern with corporeality, spatiality

DOI: 10.4324/9781003276241-5

and visuality that characterises *Une femme est une femme*, which Angéla and Émile's bathroom (partially) organises, and which this chapter will explore.

Angéla and Émile's bathroom is far from the first French bathroom that (re)organises bodies and meanings, and here we are taking a trip to the toilet with Jacques Lacan who, exhibiting the cultural fascination with our base and basic bodily functions, as well as the purported national tendency and readiness to talk about going to the loo (see Chapter 2), deploys 'the private stall offered Western man for the satisfaction of his natural needs when away from home' (Lacan 1977 [1966], 151) as a means to rewire the linguistic sign and to set up the eventual bad behaviour of the signifier (Fink 2004, 83). Principal amongst these revisions is Lacan's disenclosure of the sign which he realises by removing key graphic elements from Ferdinand de Saussure's version, specifically its circular enclosure and contested arrows, which ostensibly bind signifier and signified together and represent signification. Uprooting de Saussure's tree, Lacan also reverses the positions of the signifier and signified so that the former comes 'to dominate' the latter (80), both graphically and semantically, enabling its misbehaviour.

Lacan illustrates this bad behaviour with a set of toilet doors (Lacan 1977 [1966], 151). The simple sketch he draws upon shows two identical doors, occupying the place of the signified, pictured beneath the words 'Gentlemen' and 'Ladies', which occupy the place of the signifier. These two elements are separated by the bar. This 'duplication of signifiers' (Fink 2004, 82) forestalls the nominalist 'one-to-one correspondence between word and thing' (Lacan 1977 [1966], 149; translation modified) because it is the juxtaposition of Gentlemen and Ladies that produces 'complementary meanings' (151), which ultimately move bodies towards certain destinations according 'to the laws of urinary segregation'. Significantly, it is the delinquent signifier that moves bodies in this way because in Lacan's example 'the signifier [...] enters the signified' purportedly (and playfully), thanks to 'the squinting gaze of a near-sighted person' (translation modified) who, on approaching the doors, 'might be justified in wondering whether [...] the signifier' is reproduced on the plaques that Lacan includes in his diagram. This bathroom encounter 'seals the fate of the signified' (Fink 2004, 83), and the signifier's 'victory' over it, and establishes the conditions for the signifier later stuffing the signified; the former swells the latter's meanings. *Une femme est une femme* gets similarly stuffed.

Alongside Lacan's obvious engagement with spatiality, corporeality residually (and perhaps unexpectedly) precipitates here too and hints of the errant signifier materialise in Angéla and Émile's bathroom through the enigmatic light that fills it. This light, of course, is not without a source: it emanates from the neon signs that line the street below.[1] The street, of course, is a public space and, like cinema, it embodies the antithesis to the privacy of the bathroom. This light, then, which 'like other graphic representations of words in modern consumer culture—billboards, posters, highway signs, soap boxes'

(Hayes 2000a, 25)—constitutes a 'public vocabulary', marks an intrusion of the public into the private. Representative of a literary practice bespoke to the cityscape, across Godard's New Wave oeuvre this practice enumerates women's bodies, or at the very least their underwear brands, *O-yes Julie Poitrine*! *Toujours bleu, petit B...* emblazon the night sky here and elsewhere, for example, in *Masculin féminin* (1966). Such illuminations also make up the textual net that ultimately ensnares Michel Poiccard and are legible through Angéla and Émile's apartment windows.

When these illuminations enter their apartment via the bathroom, however, this light floats free from its original signification and arguably from signification altogether: the signifier (light) slips away (Fink 2004, 80) from the signified and takes up residence in Angéla and Émile's bathroom. Semiotically adrift, a drift that the early party sequence in *Pierrot le fou* (1965) attempts to resignify by having the guests speak in advertisingese in rooms awash with these hues, none of the characters in *Une femme est une femme* ever comment on these illuminations, further indicating an inability to reintegrate them into meaningful discourse. In a demonstration of the (Lacanian) signifier's bad behaviour, this errant, enigmatic light overwrites the bathroom's privacy with its public vocabulary. The walls of Angéla and Émile's apartment, then, 'cannot keep the street out' (Baschiera 2020, 175), and Godard's film is equally pregnable.

Godard is, of course, no stranger to citation; indeed, it is fundamental to his filmmaking practice (see Kline 1992; Godard 1999; Sterritt 1999). However, much like Émile ultimately loses the argument, Godard ultimately loses control of any incursions. Fittingly, it is Angéla and Émile's arguments that render the film especially vulnerable to getting stuffed, and when arguing about sulking, a remarkable moment of stuffing occurs via two brief shots from Agnès Varda's *L'Opéra-Mouffe* (1958) (Figure 5.1). Screened on a television set on display in a shop window, the first insert depicts Dorothée Blank lying naked on a bed, and the second, from the closing moments of Varda's film, shows

Figure 5.1 Agnès Varda's *L'Opéra-Mouffe* (1958) ostensibly trapped behind glass.

a pregnant woman trundling past a graffitied wall with shopping in hand. Subtitled *Diary of a Pregnant Woman*, the thematic parallel—pregnancy—between the two films is obvious, whilst *L'Opéra-Mouffe* combines Godard's film's concerns with corporeality and spatiality through Blank's horizontality, which is conventionally aligned with femininity, and even with animality and inhumanity (Osterweil 2014, 206; Wilson 2019, 16), and the second woman's weighty verticality. These shots, as these axial lineages suggest, do not simply refer to Varda's film in some sort of closed loop. Indeed, Emma Wilson's analysis of the sequence from which the first insert derives, entitled 'Les amoureux', inserts Blank's lived and living 'morphology' (53) into an art-historical genealogy which is in turn revitalised by this contact; it is, as Wilson describes, 'opened out' (53). For Wilson, Blank's odalisque 'echoes Velázquez's *The Rokeby Venus*' (53), whilst 'shaking up [...] the timeless still pose' (55). In so doing, 'Varda claims freedom of association and repurposing' (55) and opens out her own film to further 'kinship' (57): 'The similar poses establish parity between the subjects in Varda's stretch of meanings from satiation after love to intoxication, to sleep, unconsciousness, obliviousness and dying, all these images of the living prone' (56). In fact, Varda stretches this pose and its *vanitas* 'from the arcadia of the lovers' attachment to the brutalities and vulnerabilities of the Algerian War' (54) with such mapping realised by the graffitied skull seen in the top right corner of the frame here and later in the film—scratched onto the wall in the very moments that appear in the second insert in Godard's film (taken from the segment titled 'des angoisses').

Curiously, in Godard's edit, the diegetic frame of the first insert (the television set) excises the *vanitas*, which effectively excises Varda's marked yet subtle consciousness raising and risks confining *L'Opéra-Mouffe* to the private confines of the directors' personality and pregnancy, and even integrating Blank and the second woman into Godard's own vernacular of femininity. Indeed, in depoliticising Varda's film, Godard here arguably equates the women of Rue Mouffetard with sexuality and diminishes Varda's credibility in a similar manner to his treatment of women in *La Chinoise* (1967) (Morrey 2005, 57). Given Godard's own penchant for political graffiti as a critical part of *mise en scène* and characterisation (for instance, the young Maoists in *La Chinoise* and Paul in *Masculin féminin*), he could hardly have been indifferent to their significance in *L'Opéra-Mouffe*, and in this way, Godard surreptitiously resignifies Varda's film, which in its original iteration is patently dedicated to the resonances between the personal and the political, the private and the public, as well as to conflicting affective states (Wilson 2019, 57). Godard's edits, however, cannot contain these inserts, and they operate as an indicator of his loss of control and discreetly rewrite the male subjectivity embedded in the film's narrative. After all, it turns out that what is actually on television that evening is not *À bout de souffle*, at least not on any television that we see, but rather Varda's *L'Opéra-Mouffe*, which refuses to remain confined to its domesticated, commodified frame and instead stuffs *Une femme est une femme* in such a way that these inserts insert the film into (or, following Wilson, open it out onto) a series of specifically French socio-historico-political-corporeal contexts that the resistive opacity of women's bodies achieves, and thanks to which kinship is obtained.

Any sense of kinship seems wildly at odds with one of *Une femme est une femme*'s most famous scenes, in which Angéla and Émile, whilst ostensibly not talking to each other, argue through a careful selection of book titles. Fittingly, the bathroom is the bookend for the film's final trips to the WC and punctuates their silent squabble. In the first, Émile regards himself in the mirror. The red pulse of light illuminates him as he does so, and thereby implicates his body into the drama of the street below, much like a later scene in which his street-walking body does the work of words (Ezra 2014, 66). Accusations of squidgy soap then spark discontent between the two before teeth cleaning leads to a fragmented, incoherent exchange. The silent treatment ensues. Neither, however, can fully stifle their rage. It spills out through their chosen book covers lit by lamplight, books essentially doing the (verbal) work of bodies. *Monstre…, te faire foutre…, bourreau…, momies peruviennes…, filou…, sardine…, toutes les femmes…, au poteau*! Their war of words invites thoughts of alternative literary practices, which some of the most recent Godardian criticism encourages too. In his reappraisal of the relationship between Bazinian realism and Godard, for instance, Douglas Smith postulates the role of *collage* and *décollage* in the latter's oeuvre and how neither is as 'radically opposed to [the] essential realism' (2014, 210) André Bazin ascribes to cinema. Sticking and unsticking, gluing and ungluing, *collage* and *décollage* mobilise the real through 'integration' (214) and 'interruption' (216), respectively. Such gestures can be understood as contrastive: 'Whereas *collage* may be construed as authored, constructive and additive', Smith writes, '*décollage* presents itself as anonymous, destructive, and deductive. *Décollage* produces a discordant palimpsest of public speech from layers of assertion and contestation, whereas *collage* potentially articulates the coherent private statement of an individual artist'. Public and private are once more pitted against each other, and arguably *collage* reloads the threat of a privatised representation, which the rips and tears of *décollage* fundamentally disrespect.[2] Bypassing the mouth and the orography of the face in close-up, their astomatous exchange denies the film any (straightforward) efforts to enclose either body textually. Instead, fringed by fingers, such dactyl glimpses disclose the braided truth of the labour of textual production. Indeed, these book covers articulate *décollage*'s discordant palimpsest of public speech, treated like 'recyclable commodities', cleaned up by Godard/the close-up to acquire something of the expressivity of frontality. Their 'private lovers' quarrel' (Hayes 2000a, 25) transforms into 'a public forum' (20).

The final image here of women at the stake is especially resonant, and unsettlingly intertwines cinema and the body. It anticipates Karina's trip to the cinema in Godard's *Vivre sa vie* (1962) where, as Nana, she watches Carl Theodor Dreyer's *La Passion de Jeanne d'arc* (1928). Almost exclusively composed of close-ups, Dreyer's film style might be described as hysterical, and Karl Schoonover, in his study of Italian Neorealism, draws on Bazin's response to Dreyer's film, which foregrounds the fleshy facticity of these faces. Bazin describes it as 'a documentary of faces' (2012, 39) whereby pockmarks, pores and red patches are agents of action, whilst the tectonic and tidal qualities of wrinkles and lips that so enamoured Epstein accumulate too. The body here emerges as a secreting being, its contingencies secreting more images, both actual and metaphorical. Bodily matter produces cinema. *Vivre sa vie* literalises these secretions as we witness Nana moved to tears, through which she enters a 'mimetic' (Silverman and Farocki 1998, 11), 'mirroring relationship' with Maria Falconetti, somewhat akin to Poiccard's with Bogey, exposing the seam between fantasy and reality predicated on Karina's 'ineradicable' (29) bodily presence beneath Nana (and Angéla).

This documentary of faces, including Karina's, returns us to *Une femme est une femme* and the documentary of faces it engenders when Angéla meets Suzanne (Nicole Paquin), a recently unemployed friend who enquires about a job at the Zodiac club. Angéla initiates their chat by asking Suzanne what book she is reading, and the latter responds by embodying its title. She plays an invisible, yet audible, piano and transforms her hands into guns that fire invisible, yet audible bullets: *Tirez sur le pianiste*, Angéla correctly guesses. Once more, books mediate encounters, and when thinking about the French New Wave's missing book on bodies, *Une femme est une femme* is highly instructive because, as Suzanne's pantomime demonstrates and Kevin Hayes notes (2000b, 70), the film equates the two; '[t]he female body is [...] analogous to the bookcover' (see also Ezra [2014, 68–9]). We witness further evidence for this immediately before Angéla and Suzanne's meeting when Alfred asks a woman at the bar, who happens to be Jeanne Moreau, how things are with 'Jules et Jim'? *Moderato*, she replies, without the implied *cantabile*—another of Godard's subtle omissions. Here, then, the repressed irrigation of French New Wave films by literature resonates and forms a *collage*. For Jules and Jim are, of course, Moreau's lovers in the film of the same name, whilst Moreau and Belmondo star in the film adaptation of Marguerite Duras's novel which is partially eclipsed here. Belmondo thus meets Moreau, and in doing so, Henri-Pierre Roché meets Marguerite Duras, and François Truffaut meets Peter Brooks, with Moreau the impure glue of this *collage* of literary and cinematic encounters. Following Belmondo and Moreau's brief encounter, the film quickly loses interest in Angéla and Suzanne's bodies and books, and instead starts to explore the Parisian pavement. A patchwork of different faces materialises that reveals the contingencies of the flesh—young, old, white, black, male, female, similar, different—and these faces are scored by Angéla and Suzanne's conversation, first about the striptease and then their (ex-) lovers' bodies, with talk of Alfred's shoulders and Émile's knees floating above these anonymous mugs (Figure 5.2). Their discussion intertwines the public and the private, the actual and the imaginary to form an erotic itinerary whereby a pseudo-documentary aesthetic breaches the film's already precarious generic

Of bathroom sinks and the streets below 47

Figure 5.2 Women talking: Angèla (Anna Karina) and Suzanne's (Nicole Paquin) voices float above anonymous mugs.

Figure 5.3 Women talking: Anonymous mugs on the Rue Mouffetard in Agnès Varda's *L'Opéra-Mouffe* (1958).

hybridity. Like the enigmatic lights that thin and limn Angéla and Émile's apartment walls, these faces represent the city life that limns their story and thins the walls of Godard's film.

This breach, caused by this documentary of faces, returns us to *L'Opéra-Mouffe* because the many faces that we see here echo the many faces that make up Varda's film, and which Godard's earlier citation ignores. Nonetheless, the two films here assemble a *collage* that comments on their respective erotic itineraries (Figure 5.3). In the first instance, Angéla and Suzanne ventriloquise the old women who we see silently talking at the beginning of *L'Opéra-Mouffe*. We can only imagine what the latter pairings are discussing with animated intensity. Perhaps they too are talking about their lovers' bodies. This doubling confirms discourse as the only intercourse in *Une femme est une femme*—a chastity reinforced by the pre- and apparently post-coital chats that litter the film and which *L'Opéra-Mouffe*'s openly intimate and communicative couplings place into sharp relief. Whereas *L'Opéra-Mouffe* is the crucible for Varda's New Wave corporeality, *Une femme est une femme* frequently dematerialises the body through speech, text, image and allusion. Like Varda, however, Godard grounds his documentary of faces in a recognisable part of Paris, the tenth arrondissement, via shots of the Porte Saint-Denis. Given this area's long associations with prostitution, such remapping attempts to insert this documentary of faces into a distinctly Godardian vernacular. Prostitution, after all, soon becomes the principal mode of contemporary French living in Godard's later New Wave period and beyond (see Mulvey and MacCabe 1980; Loshitzky 1995).

Alongside pregnancy, the predominance of elderly faces is perhaps what draws the two films closest together, but equally what brands the breach that this documentary of faces enacts as decidedly 'Vardadian' (Mayer 2019). Indeed, this breach marks the signifier, *L'Opéra-Mouffe*, as being out of its Godardian bounds. Here the film sheds its televisual frame, or enclosure, and thus disenclosed it stuffs *Une femme est une femme* by creating a gallery of types (Beugnet 2006, 31)—a representational strategy that Martine Beugnet identifies with Varda's oeuvre, and in particular with her 'neighbourhood documentaries' (28). Through repetition, Varda 'challenge[s] the conventional principles of' (33) agency, exposition, scrutiny and fetishism associated with the close-up and across her filmography the close-up is something of a 'motif' (29) that marries the corporeal changes wrought by pregnancy and ageing. In its takeover of *Une femme est une femme*, *L'Opéra-Mouffe* rewires the agency conventionally associated with the close-up. Here such agency does not reside in the images, like some token for identification, but rather generates the very substance of Godard's film, and this agentic matrix destabilises Godard's authorial control. Indeed, it summons the film's anxious caress, which is once again triggered by the real of the body—a realness that Blank and the flower-munching mother-to-be underwrite—yet sublimated via editing rather than *mise en scène* by characters. Accordingly, the ostensibly phlegmatic *collage* constituted from a cascade of New Wave texts and bodies that Belmondo's meeting with Moreau occasions instead comes to compensate for an erosion of the French New Wave's purported male exceptionalism. The shots of the Porte Saint-Denis seek to do likewise, whilst the frenzy of close-ups of Angéla that closes this section of the film seals its vulnerability. These close-ups are meant to contain any threat, but read alongside Poiccard's hollowness and Paul's exteriority, this montage signifies Godard's desperation and desire to regain control.

As Angéla and Suzanne talk, the visual- and soundtrack showcase the body in its most mundanely public and most intimately private moments, which collapse the public and the private, the social body and the physical body. The stake is a similar site of conflation. Joan of Arc was, as Dreyer's film depicts, burnt at the stake for heresy. The public nature of her execution collapses spectacle onto social cleansing, in much the same way as tonsuring in the aftermath of the Second World War sought to cleanse and reclaim the spaces and subjectivities of nationhood and community at the expense of women's bodies. Questions of (normative) hygiene return us to the bathroom, and questions of public display once more problematise its privacy. *Au poteau*, the intimacy between the physical body and the social body is exposed; *au cinéma*, we encounter a similar exposure whereby the cinematic body embodies this seam. Such intimacy, then, is essentially inherent in cinema-going. Angéla's third and final trip to the bathroom offers something of a riposte to this intimacy, whilst giving rise to a specifically French socio-historico-political-corporeal context. During this visit, she attempts to shower only to be thwarted by an absence of water, and is then interrupted by a phone call. As she disrobes—bearing the promise of feminine undress that was once cinematically coincident with the bathroom—Angéla turns from the audience, lifts her nightdress and arches her back to form a denuded, headless, abstract, fleshy expanse. We witness the work of the musculature beneath the epidermis, the twitches of her spine and shoulder blades as she wriggles out of her nightgown. Balázsian signifiers of the real, these jerks are not the only rebellion that Angéla's back knits into the film. After all, her posteriority echoes and upends Varda's *Rokeby Venus*, suggesting that the threat to Godard comes not only from interlopers but from within too.

In a cross section of European art cinema, Brandon Colvin considers the significatory potential of the back. Under what he terms 'dorsality', Colvin categorises a *mise en scène* that privileges the back over the face as a further distinguishing mark of art cinema corporeality's 'deviations from classical norms' (2017, 193). In particular, he unpacks how such 'dorsal staging' (192) brings about 'compositional defamiliarization' (195) as well as 'denial' (199). The former imposes a 'deliberate figural objectification' onto on-screen bodies, whilst the latter withholds interiority, 'signal[ling] a state of self-absorption, of self-assessment, a sense of thoughts under collection in privacy'. The sight of Angéla's back, of course, foreshadows her later Godardian incarnation as Nana (and Macha Méril's in *Une femme mariée* [1964]), yet her exposed epidermis is equally reminiscent of Alain Resnais and Marguerite Duras's *Hiroshima mon amour* (1959) and its cinematography and *mise en scène* that centre on the body (Moore 2005, 663). Opening with close-ups of an illegible assortment of body parts, embracing and intertwining, Resnais's film initially only offers up flesh; arguably, even bodies come later. Most legible amongst this medley is a naked back gripped by hands in a manner that recalls Angéla and Émile's bickering book covers. Yet it is not simply the lovers' bodies that Resnais's film is concerned with, for it is seen as a 'crucial vector of memory' (Banaji 2012, 21) in the history of *les tondues*: women found guilty of 'horizontal collaboration'. Through the machinations of cinema—most notably a series of flashbacks that transition via various body parts—the private history of Emmanuelle Riva's Elle is rendered public, and what the film thus makes especially intelligible is the intertwining of 'gender, visuality and historical memory' (Moore 2005, 658) which establishes a cephalic regime that codes shameful episodes of French history as aberrant via women's bodies. The brutalised, suffering, imperiled, injured bodies that populate the images of *les tondues*, and that we are left with by virtue of the carefully choreographed Resistance counter-narrative, seal this seam, and through 'ubiquitous reproduction' (659), these images join the ranks of the public vocabulary of modern consumer culture, which here feminise *la belle France* and fix 'her' as a passive and penetrated body (660). However, in kinship with the indecipherable fleshy jumble that opens *Hiroshima mon amour*, the epidermal expanse of Angéla's back disrupts this register, joins the ranks of 'a writing style that powerfully transgresses dominant cinematic codes' (Sellier 2008, 214) and 'creates an organic and valorized connection [...] between the feminine and aesthetic innovation' that is often overlooked, or denied, but which Resnais and Duras's film nurtures.

This harmonious disruption, or disruptive kinship, takes place by means of a subtle interplay of visuality, corporeality and orality, for Angéla's headless verso rips her body from the easy legibility of public vocabulary (Figure 5.4). The verticality of the *mise en scène* that Angéla's back orchestrates—embedded in the showerhead and the hanging curtain, towels and dressing gown—overwrites the relentless horizontality assigned to femininity. On the precipice of a striptease, and thus on the precipice of revealing her discursive and anatomical lack, the female body again appears to be at risk. But her dorsality means that there is no mouth around which allusions to the female

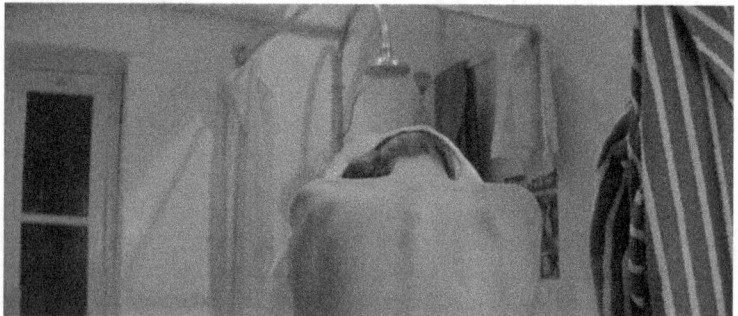

Figure 5.4 Angéla's disruptive dorsality.

genitals and the male gaze can precipitate. Refusing a seamless synchronization of voice and body, no proprietorial striptease occurs, which denies cinema its easy symbolic divestiture (Silverman 1988, 50). Angéla's back thus literalises a rhetoric of refusal: a refusal to have her physical body co-opted and spectacularised by the social body, and by cabalistically conjuring the dorsal compositions that have structured this chapter, as if a hieroglyph, she is not alone in this refusal. Standing alone here, though, her body does things to the profilmic. It irons out the recessive quality of the bathroom, an ecstasy her body promotes, thanks to its interruptive presence. As the intrusive light slips signification, Angéla's back slips diegetic interiority and, in solidarity with the women silenced by the public vocabulary of mass consumer culture, it secretes an astomatous cry: *Toutes les femmes...au poteau...va te faire foutre!*

Notes

1 According to Richard Neupert (2007), this light's ultimate source is Hollywood musicals (34), while the film's Paul Klee-inspired palette could be read as a discreet nod to *Le Petit Soldat* (1960).
2 The activism and discordant palimpsests of public speech of *Les Colleuses*, who plaster posters across French cities decrying violence against women, extend the work of *décollage* (see Wilsher 2021).

References

Banaji, Ferzina. 2012. *France, Film and The Holocaust*. New York: Palgrave Macmillan.
Baschiera, Stefano. 2020. "At Home with the Nouvelle Vague: Apartment Plots and Domestic Urbanism in Godard's *Une femme est une femme* and Varda's *Cléo de 5 à 7*." In *Film and Domestic Space: Architectures, Representations, Dispositif*, edited by Stefano Baschiera and Miriam de Rosa, 171–87. Edinburgh: Edinburgh University Press.
Beugnet, Martine. 2006. "Close-up Vision: Re-mapping the Body in the Work of Contemporary French Women Filmmakers." *Nottingham French Studies* 45 (3): 24–38.
Colvin, J. Brandon. 2017. "The Other Side of Frontality: Dorsality in European Art Cinema." *New Review of Film and Television Studies* 15 (2): 191–210.
Ezra, Elizabeth. 2014. "*Un femme est infâme*: Godard's Writing Lesson." In *A Companion to Jean-Luc Godard*, edited by Tom Conley and T. Jefferson Kline, 60–70. Oxford: Wiley-Blackwell.
Fink, Bruce. 2004. *Lacan to the Letter: Reading Ecrits Closely*. Saint Paul: University of Minnesota Press.
Godard, Jean-Luc. 1999. *JLG/JLG*. Paris: P.O.L.
Hayes, Kevin J. 2000a. "Bookcover as Intertitle in the Cinema of Jean-Luc Godard." *Visible Language* 34 (1): 14–31.
Hayes, Kevin J. 2000b. "*Une Femme Est une Femme*: A Modern Woman's Bookshelf." *Film Criticism* 25 (1): 65–82.
Kline, T. Jefferson. 1992. *Screening the Text: Intertextuality in French New Wave Cinema*. Baltimore: The Johns Hopkins University Press.

Lacan, Jacques. 1977 [1966]. *Écrits: A Selection*. Translated by Alan Sheridan. London: Tavistock Publications.
Loshitzky, Yosefa. 1995. *The Radical Faces of Godard and Bertolucci*. Detroit: Wayne State University Press.
Mayer, So. 2019. "The Varda Variations: (Re)introductions of the Auteure in *Documenteur* and Beyond." *cléo: a journal of film and feminism* <https://cleojournal.com/2018/04/11/varda-variations-documenteur/>
Moore, Alison. 2005. "History, Memory, and Trauma in Photography of the *Tondues*: Visuality of the Vichy Past through the Silent Image of Women." *Gender and History* 17 (3): 657–81.
Morrey, Douglas. 2005. *Jean-Luc Godard*. Manchester: Manchester University Press.
Mulvey, Laura and Colin MacCabe. 1980. "Images of Women, Images of Sexuality." In *Godard: Images, Sounds, Politics*, edited by Colin MacCabe, 79–104. London: The MacMillan Press.
Neupert, Richard. 2007. *A History of the French New Wave Cinema* (Second Edition). Madison: University of Wisconsin Press.
Osterweil, Ara. 2014. *Flesh Cinema: The Corporeal Turn in American Avant-Garde Film*. Manchester: Manchester University Press.
Schoonover, Karl. 2012. *Brutal Vision: The Neorealist Body in Postwar Italian Cinema*. Minneapolis: University of Minnesota Press.
Sellier, Geneviève. 2008. *Masculine Singular: French New Wave Cinema*. Translated by Kristin Ross. Durham: Duke University Press.
Silverman, Kaja. 1988. *The Acoustic Mirror: The Female Voice in Psychoanalysis and Cinema*. Bloomington: Indiana University Press.
Silverman, Kaja and Harun Farocki. 1998. *Speaking about Godard*. New York: New York University Press.
Smith, Douglas. 2014. *"(Dé)collage:* Bazin, Godard, Aragon." In *A Companion to Jean-Luc Godard*, edited by Tom Conley and T. Jefferson Kline, 210–23. Oxford: Wiley-Blackwell.
Sterritt, David. 1999. *The Films of Jean-Luc Godard: Seeing the Invisible*. Cambridge: Cambridge University Press.
Wilsher, Kim. 2021. "'No More Shame': The French Women Breaking the Law to Highlight Femicide." *Guardian* <https://www.theguardian.com/world/2021/mar/23/no-more-shame-the-french-women-breaking-the-law-to-highlight-femicide>
Wilson, Emma. 2019. *The Reclining Nude: Agnès Varda, Catherine Breillat, and Nan Goldin*. Liverpool: Liverpool University Press.

6 Of wigs and fig leaves

Flashes of a woman's back realise a similar rhetoric of refusal in *Le Mépris* (1963), and despite Brigitte Bardot's Camille being afflicted by a relentless horizontality throughout—recumbent on beds, sofas, roofs like a postmodern odalisque—the film often refuses the straightforward scopophilia of the male gaze (Mulvey 1975). In the early bedroom sequence, for instance, in which Bardot's prone body takes centre stage, the kaleidoscopic filters Godard employs rhetorically stage this refusal. Here, Camille unambiguously draws attention to her body and embarks upon a 'verbal dismemberment' (Macaux 2014, 131), prefacing the violence to come, her 'corporeal inventory' serving her (body) up as an easily consumable visual commodity. Through a self-blazoning gesture of auto-anatomization, she becomes feet, ankles, knees, thighs, bum, breasts, nipples, shoulders and finally a face, and successfully aims any sense of contempt firmly at the industrial-economic machine (Silverman and Farocki 1998, 34). This auto-atomisation and authorship is not the only writing that Bardot does in the film. However, in these moments, this apparent rhetoric of refusal inscribes her body into the most faithful book about women's bodies in Godard's New Wave films, a confusing tome that cleaves contradictions. In paying lip service to Godard's producers, Bardot launders his contempt, suggesting that her carnal catalogue overlooks a critical, orifical body part: mouthpiece. There is, moreover, another body part missing from Camille's list, one that sits discreetly within the erotic inventory of Bardot's body and that slips into and out of view when she asks, *Et mes fesses?* Secreted here is the anus, perhaps the most anxiety-inducing of all orifices, and certainly the most closely aligned with the loss of control associated with the bathroom. Like depictions of Godardian femininity, the anus represents something of a double bind. It is, according to William Ian Miller, 'indelibly the lowest-status place on the body, rendered disgusting by feces and buffoonish and comical by gas' (1998, 100), and yet it can 'bring down the whole body, making it subservient to the anal' (99). Democratic, yet apparently all-powerful, the anus is also 'a relational term', necessarily propping up 'what rests on top of it [which] needs its grounding, needs its support [...] so as to enable the very possibility of highness and superiority.

DOI: 10.4324/9781003276241-6

[...] It must be secured or everything else built upon it crumbles' (100–1). The anus thus organises corporeal and sociocultural schemas and, consequently, it becomes tempting and teasing, 'the gateway to the most private, to the most personal space of all' (101), like Camille's backside, yet 'contaminating' (100) like Godard's treatment of women when his films reproduce what they seek to critique (Mulvey and MacCabe 1980, 103). Despite its anal reticence, illustrated by the coyness of *fesses*, *Le Mépris* is an object lesson in Godardian contamination, illustrated by Bardot's humiliations and Camille's death (Loshitzky 1995, 138; Sellier 2008, 208). This chapter will thus join existing discussions of how anality organises Godard's representation of women during his New Wave period (Mulvey and MacCabe 1980; Loshitzky 1995; Silverman and Farocki 1998). However, whereas existing work prefers the bedroom to the bathroom and ties anality to sexuality, consumerism or both (for example, *Week-end* [1967] and *Deux ou trois choses que je sais d'elle* [1967]), this discussion will centre the bathroom and examine how the 'undeniable connection' (Miller 1998, 96) that '[t]he mouth and the anus bear' is not only an anatomical and sociocultural truism but a Godardian one too.

In another lengthy domestic sequence—over 30 minutes—during which both Camille and Paul (Michel Piccoli) bathe, *Le Mépris* readily establishes the interrelationship between books, bodies and the bathroom, with Camille reading a book about Fritz Lang in the bath, which 'refracts the "real" (Lang) through the "artificial" (the fictive world of the film)' (Macaux 2014, 135), recouping the nestling of fantasy and reality and restaging the fantasy of the bathroom mirror. As she bathes, Paul flicks through a book on Greek antiquity that is chock-full of intertwining bodies, and the film later pushes this interrelationship to parodic extremes when Camille sunbathes with a book fig-leafed on her derriere. This handy sunscreen hints at the seam between the literary and anality which finds a series of expressions throughout the film, including via the black wig that toggles Camille between icon and mere mortal. When donning the wig, Camille receives a slap from Paul, a cruel testament to her corporeality, and her shock at his violence is recorded in a lengthy close-up. When divested of this hairpiece, she is shown in a more abstract close-up in the bathroom, reciting profanity (Figures 6.1 and 6.2). Emblematic of French New Wave corporeality, these close-ups form a seam and are also illustrative of the film's anal reticence, for the face in close-up sanitises the body's secretions, despite the excesses it houses and the hieroglyphic potentiality it possesses, whilst staining *Le Mépris* with a distinguishing mark of national cinema. This fundament of French New Wave style and corporeality, however, soon becomes imbricated with the fundament by transforming the face into a conduit for the lowest of literary practices: graffiti.

In the first instance, these close-ups reload the workings of *collage* and *décollage*. The wig is destructive and interruptive. It anonymises and tears Bardot's star image from the easy legibility of public vocabulary, rendering her body

Of wigs and fig leaves 55

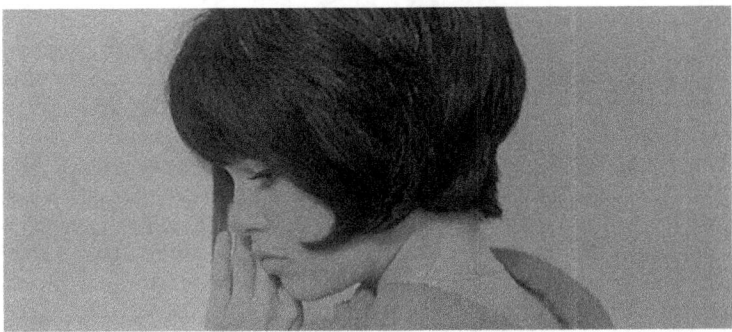

Figure 6.1 Camille (Brigitte Bardot) donning her black wig.

Figure 6.2 Camille reciting profanity in the bathroom.

something of a discordant palimpsest. We know it is Bardot beneath the wig, but her image on-screen does not chime with our expectations and in fact recalls Anna Karina in *Vivre sa vie* (1962). Following *À bout de souffle* (1960), it reminds us of the true labour of textual production—inscription upon inscription upon inscription—yet (again perhaps reassuringly) narrows its stakes to an exclusively Godardian frame of reference. Once again, Camille becomes a Godardian mouthpiece, embarking on one of his favourite literary practices: citation (see Kline 1992; Godard 1999; Sterritt 1999). Yet this black bob is not Karina's hair; it merely stands in for it in Godard's dissection of prostitution. Indeed, across Godard's New Wave oeuvre, Karina's hair is very plastic. In *Le Petit Soldat* (1960), for example, she incessantly plays with it during the photography sequence, scooping it up, letting it hang and effectively defying Michel Subor's attempts to fix her image, whilst she sports all manner of hairstyles in *Une Femme est une Femme* (1961), *Bande à part* (1964) and *Pierrot le fou* (1965): pigtails, ponytails, half up-half down, space buns, etc. The artificiality of Bardot's hair thus points up the artificiality of Karina's, and such dynamic inscriptions subtly destabilise Godard's authorship. Further inscriptions of Karina's do in Godard's New Wave films do likewise, thanks to a two-dimensional cameo in *Deux ou trois choses que je sais d'elle*. Here Karina and her hair appear in poster form, ostensibly as Nana. Yet she wears the same fur-lined (blue) dress in *Une femme est une femme* (as well as something similar in *Alphaville* [1965]). Hair and costume thus risk being misaligned, and such clumsy *collage* means that Godard's principal modus operandi stalls, which yet more follicular hijinks exacerbate. Back in blonde, Camille's swearing is both additive and constructive: it authors an alternative inscription of her star image, allowing her to articulate a different sense of self much like the wig enabled. Thus, it creates. She refuses to shut up and be pretty and thus rejects the image imposed upon her by others (see also Macaux [2014, 132]; Morrey [2005, 19]). Enunciated in isolation, her swearing parallels the book titles in *Une femme est une femme*—marooned blocks of language that seemingly make no sense, a superfluous bodily secretion for which the bathroom is a haven. We might imagine these secretions sketched out next to Camille's head in swollen, supersized letters like graffiti, and it is through her bathroom protest that the bottom starts to dominate the top.

Graffiti, an 'alternative' literary practice (Fieni 2012, 74), is very much at home in the bathroom where, before erupting onto the more visible spaces of the city, walls, subway cars and white vans in what Jean Baudrillard describes as a kind of 'savage offensive' (2007 [1993], 76), it 'constituted the basest form (the sexual and pornographic base), the shameful, repressed inscriptions in pissoirs and waste grounds' (Baudrillard 2007 [1993], 79), as what Alan Dundes termed 'latrinalia' (1966, 238). The aerosol of Camille's breath here deputises for those that more typically take the state to task by tagging its structures, which produces one of graffiti's structuring overlaps, here between 'the letters of graffiti [and] the letter of the law' (Fieni 2012, 75):

> by definition, the graffitist positions him or herself outside the law, while also writing on the very material surfaces of the law (property, the walls built by the state); graffiti does not simply stand outside or against the state, but always links up with the state, disfigures the representatives of the state, and becomes barred by state science.

Echoing her opening blazon, Camille's delinquent anatomisation territorialises the wall and collapses the loftiness of the head/mouthpiece onto the lowliness of the anal by disinterring this base literary practice, whilst briefly sinking Godard's film towards the shameful depths of pissoirs and waste grounds and transforming the cinema screen into a toilet wall (see Baudrillard 2007 [1993], 79; Fieni 2012, 79). In doing so, Camille confuses hers and Godard's positions. Who here is the ass (lowly yet omnipotent) and who is the mouthpiece (subservient yet celebrated), or are they one and the same? Alongside repression, repetition and ritual also inform graffiti, and Camille's latrinalia, which Yosefa Loshitzky categorises as a 'long litany of names by which women were called in the Middle Ages' (1995, 141), collides with the 'subversive litany of anonymity' (Baudrillard 2007 [1993], 84) that characterises graffiti. Who are these harlots, who, unknown yet unchanging, stubbornly travel across the centuries and survive waves of feminism? This collision challenges some of the fundamental facets of graffiti, most notably its anonymity, mutability and ephemerality (Fieni 2012, 74), as well as the structures of Godard's cinema. Graffiti is always vulnerable to editing or even erasure. It is always a work in progress and 'never a product, always production' (75). When donning the wig, Camille flirts with the anonymity graffiti centres and attempts to extend this trait when reciting her own subversive litany (see Baudrillard 2007 [1993]; Fieni 2012, 75). This anonymising self-authorship, however, is only partially successful. Bardot and Karina insist *à fleur d'image*. Equally, the timelessness of Camille's tags opposes such vulnerability, whilst attempting to take ownership of them by overwriting the film's opening *collage* of desire with arseholes, scum and shit, anticipating Godard's later 'anal theme' (Loshitzky 1995, 139). Bodily matter produces cinema. In becoming vulnerable to editing, Godard becomes graffiti, yet he also becomes a graffiti artist.

The overlap between different Godardian incarnations of Karina, which a bewigged Bardot highlights, attests as much. For in moving from body to body across Godard's New Wave films, disrespecting the distinctions between them, Karina's hair/image becomes something of a 'mobile script' (Fieni 2012, 77) and embodies the 'polymorphous perversity' (Baudrillard 2007 [1993], 82) of graffiti and its 'run[ning] from one house to the next, from one wall of a building to the next, from the wall onto the window or the door, or windows on subway trains, or the pavements'. The distinct stages of Godard's filmography suggest likewise, especially his experiments with dialectical thinking and montage in *Histoire(s) du cinéma* (1988–98) where once again the surface is critical, time is spatialised, and space is temporalized. For, like the graffitied wall that 'enter[s] into improvised collaboration with other writers' (Fieni 2012, 75) and consequently records many different 'durations', the 'non-linear approach to history' (Silverman 2013, 27) that Godard comes to adopt means that 'events [depicted] are "piled up" one on the other rather than ordered in a chain'.

Pile-ups drive Camille's latrinalia into the not so anally reticent, anti-establishment diatribe of *Week-end*, which in many ways operates as a distorted mirror image of *Le Mépris*. Indeed, in a warped reflection of Camille's self-blazon, early in *Week-end* a poorly lit Corinne catalogues an orifice, orb and dairy-rich orgy she recently participated in for her lover. Graffiti would thus very much be at home in the toilet of a film that *Week-end* undoubtedly is. An anarchic road movie (Hayward 2005, 252), the fatal car crashes that structure the film are merely a symptom of a worldview, indeed its worldview,

58 Of wigs and fig leaves

where everything turns to shit. Accordingly, the anus, 'signifier of equivalence' (Silverman and Farocki 1998, 89) between bodies and 'excrement', shapes its world whereby the correlation between consumerism and defecation becomes even more obvious in what Harun Farocki and Kaja Silverman call 'anal capitalism':

> In late capitalism, the commodity quickly gives way to "waste." [...] With this serialization of the exchange process, the moment of enjoyment of each new commodity also becomes briefer and briefer, so that it passes for this reason as well much more quickly into the category of "shit."
> (89–90)

Road movie and anality crash when Corinne and Roland finally arrive at their destination, Oinville, bringing the advertised road trip to an end. Vaulting off the bin lorry that has ferried them on the final leg of their journey, the pair briefly abandon the inheritance plot for a bath, and as they dash towards Corinne's mother's house, WEEKEND flashes on-screen unencumbered. Its first appearance at the beginning of the film postdates mention of its 'cosmic scrap heap' (Silverman and Farocki 1998, 111) and later instances are seen in conjunction with other titles, such as dates. Next, we see Corinne batheing, whilst an off-screen Roland reads an unflattering blazon about the hippopotamus who, wishing to live in water, is condemned to fan out his own shit with his tail to prove his honour (see also Sterritt 1999, 118) (Figure 6.3). Perhaps befitting the contrarian logic of the film, instead of graffiti the bathroom in *Week-end* supplements the imaginary museum that Godard's

Figure 6.3 Corinne (Mireille Darc) in the bath.

filmography constructs and in fact features an 'Old Master' painting of a shorthaired brunette (a hint of Karina?) with her left breast exposed, who 'engage[s] in a culturally idealized female activity: washing herself' (105). Juxtaposed with Corinne's batheing, the film here produces a mini *mise en abyme*, and for all its nonconformity *Week-end* checks off several items on the bodily agenda of the bathroom (washing, bathing, soaking, shitting [in voice-off], looking in the mirror, picking spots, reading damp books and no sex) and, through its painterly allusions, it overwrites the polymorphous perversity of the anus (and graffiti) and redoes gender. In a world defined by deviousness, debauchery and degradation, the bathroom temporarily stems this overall decline and stalls the metaphorical decline that the water closet signifies across Godard's New Wave oeuvre where it almost outlasts the car. Indeed, considering what prefaces and follows its appearance—orgies, fatal car crashes, rape, immolation, robberies, kidnappings and cannibalism—the film here paints a convincing yet incongruous domestic scene. They even say *I love you* and I believe them.

Week-end's trip to the bathroom also integrates scenes of provincial life. Presumably ordered by Corinne's mother to hurry up, adding further accent to the film's fleeting domesticity, the visualtrack abandons the bathroom and offers a brief and uninspiring portrait of Oinville: a road, a wall, a church and a poster for Total oil. The soundtrack, however, remains attuned to the bathroom, and Roland's reading and Camille's sploshing and demands that he listen to her score these images of village life. We next see Corinne for a final time in the bath, and a fade transitions into two familiar titles—a film adrift in the cosmos and found on a scrapheap—followed by a final pastoral scene. These titles telescope to the film's beginning, whilst a second fade transitions into a scene of Roland attempting to barter with Corinne's mother for a share of the inheritance. Her refusal leads to her violent murder, which displaces the whole bloody microcinema attached to the cinematic bathroom, as well as its elimination, onto the skinned rabbit gifted by a Monsieur Flaubert. Waves of blood wash over its carcass, pooling in its eye socket, which blindly stares back at us and evokes the insistent gazes of the anonymous brunette in the painting, and the anonymous blonde on the Total Oil poster, that bear down on audiences in another orgy of orbs and orifices that this time implicates, rather than excludes, the spectator. With a plan in place for the disposal of Corinne's mother's body, the pair flee Oinville in a yellow convertible.

The bathroom in *Week-end* thus maps different parts of the film. Indeed, it possesses the weakest of gravitational pulls before the rest of the film floats off into the cosmos and drifts towards the scrapheap. Indeed, this scene might be said to constitute *Week-end*, which emerges as nothing more than a road trip to the bathroom. It could be argued that the film does not really begin until Corinne's initial mention of the bathroom, for this is the first time its title enjoys some exclusive screen time, and the bathroom constitutes our despicable duo's final destination, whilst Godard ends his time with narrative cinema in the smallest room in the house. After all, once Corinne and Roland flee Oinville, the film breaks down into an increasingly chaotic series of vignettes that once again betray Godard's 'critical intentions' (Loshitzky 1995, 146) by 'add[ing] new, original images to the museum of the degradation of women', including the image of a woman's legs scissored in the air as a fish is inserted into her vagina. If anality does in fact organise the presiding political economy of late capitalism, then the bathroom is the perfect location for the final smouldering embers of civilization.

Finality, anality and Godardian femininity thus intimately intersect, and across *Le Mépris* and *Week-end* these endings concern the end of world, the end of cinema, the end of French New Wave corporeality as we know it and the end of lovemaking, which returns us to *Le Mépris*. As Paul mopes over the prospect of no longer being able to sleep with his wife, Camille facetiously proffers herself, as long as he's quick about it. Her flash of flesh triggers a cascade of images that centre on Camille and Paul's relationship, including the film's famous naked inserts, which Loshitzky damningly reads as akin to photos for the family album of babies 'with their backsides up' (1995, 139) (Figure 6.4). Bardot here is prone on blue, white and red, which, like the stake, distastefully collapses the physical and social body, fetishising and spectacularising the former, whilst feminising the latter. Here she is oneiric, yet fleshy. Decontextualised and contextualised, corporealised and decorporealised, she is also largely decapitated. Her acephalic status is significant because it means that her corporeality is not sublimated by a focus on the face. Instead, the anus organises these inserts. In this way, in the presiding corporeal vernacular of the French New Wave, her body appears almost gratuitously excessive, an insincere over-inscription à la Anita Ekberg.

The over-inscription of Bardot's backside further overwrites the film's opening *collage* of desire through its (accidentally) hyperbolic intertwining of femininity and abjection, and the body here is verb in its refusal to sanitise the profilmic by means of the close-up. In this refusal, it hyperbolises and

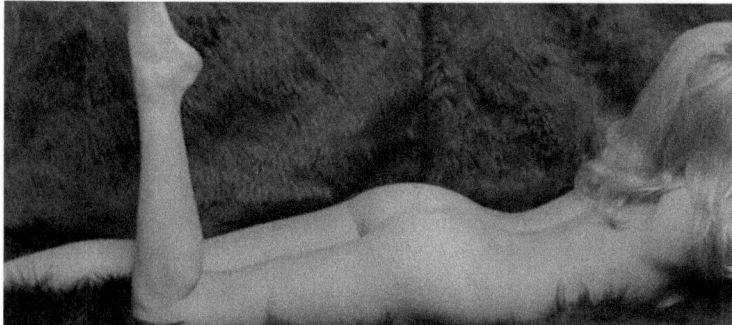

Figure 6.4 A decapitated Camille in no-man's land.

ridicules the male gaze, thanks to its own hyperbolisation. In this refusal, and through its excessiveness, it showcases the contingencies of the flesh in the form of an uneven tan. Bikini bottom or book cover, who knows? The body on-screen always transports something of the amateur that signals a lack of authorial control and threatens corporeal excess. It thus disrupts the threat of the ahistorical eternal connoted by the statue seen intermittently throughout the scene with the accidental and the everyday (see de Beauvoir 1959). It foregrounds the body as bending, as hinged, an obscenity which disrupts the smooth perfection of Bardot's skin. At leisure, the body is very much at risk of co-option. It appears hypervulnerable in its hypervisuality. Indeed, what this flash of flesh does to the profilmic here is to take it into the riskiest and most recessive of all gendered, cinematic spaces: the no-man's land that exists outside of narrative time and space, above which Paul and Camille's disembodied voices float (see Mulvey 1975). Once more, an interplay of visuality, corporeality and orality converges. Degraded, here she is cinema, her cheeks the currency of a notably misogynistic strain, caught within the dirt and detritus of mass culture, of which cinema, and its diegetic, psychic and corporeal closets, is perhaps the filthiest constituent part. Desynchronised, however, Camille refuses to stay recessive. Decapitated, France's ersatz Marianne deposes the hold that the nation state has long held on French women's heads and, much like Angéla's dorsality in *Une femme est une femme*, Camille's anality enacts a riposte to the libidinally cathected gendered visuality of the French New Wave, in the process farting out Godard, who at least momentarily experiences the loss of (bowel) control associated with the bathroom. The scrambling of the Tricolore's running order further undermines any domestic claims on women's bodies. Acephalic, the unencumbered display of her shoulders, her back(side), her elbows, her knees and her feet deracinates the fig leaf, and, thus deterritorialized, the inscription of Bardot's body in its more private moments and parts materialises as agentic, appropriative, disruptive and resistant. It demonstrates that in Godard's New Wave films sometimes you're the arse, and sometimes you're the mouthpiece, and sometimes the arse and the mouthpiece are one and the same, especially if your body is a woman's, and that sometimes it is women's bodies that trump the arsery of authorial control. *Alors, tu trouves que ça me va toujours mal*? *C'est ta faute*.

References

Baudrillard, Jean. 2007 [1993]. *Symbolic Exchange and Death*. Translated by Iain Hamilton Grant. Los Angeles: SAGE Publications.
de Beauvoir, Simone. 1959. *Brigitte Bardot and the Lolita Syndrome*. Translated by Bernard Fretchman. London: Four Square.
Dundes, Alan. 1966. "The American Concept of Folklore." *Journal of the Folklore Institute* 3 (3): 226–49.

Fieni, David. 2012. "What a Wall Wants, Or How Graffiti Thinks: Nomad Grammatology in the French Banlieue." *Diacritics* 40 (2): 72–93.
Godard, Jean-Luc. 1999. *JLG/JLG*. Paris: P.O.L.
Hayward, Susan. 2005. *French National Cinema* (Second Edition). Abingdon: Routledge.
Kline, T. Jefferson. 1992. *Screening the Text: Intertextuality in French New Wave Cinema*. Baltimore: The Johns Hopkins University Press.
Loshitzky, Yosefa. 1995. *The Radical Faces of Godard and Bertolucci*. Detroit: Wayne State University Press.
Macaux, Emily. 2014. "A Postmodern Consideration of Jean-Luc Godard's *Le Mépris*." In *A Companion to Jean-Luc Godard*, edited by Tom Conley and T. Jefferson Kline, 128–42. Oxford: Wiley-Blackwell.
Miller, Willian Ian. 1998. *The Anatomy of Disgust*. Cambridge: Harvard University Press.
Morrey, Douglas. 2005. *Jean-Luc Godard*. Manchester: Manchester University Press.
Mulvey, Laura. 1975. "Visual Pleasure and Narrative Cinema." *Screen* 16 (3): 6–18.
Mulvey, Laura and Colin MacCabe. 1980. "Images of Women, Images of Sexuality." In *Godard: Images, Sounds, Politics*, edited by Colin MacCabe, 79–104. London: The MacMillan Press.
Sellier, Geneviève. 2008. *Masculine Singular: French New Wave Cinema*. Translated by Kristin Ross. Durham: Duke University Press.
Silverman, Kaja and Harun Farocki. 1998. *Speaking about Godard*. New York: New York University Press.
Silverman, Max. 2013. *Palimpsestic Memory: The Holocaust and Colonialism in French and Francophone Fiction and Film*. New York: Berghahn Books.
Sterritt, David. 1999. *The Films of Jean-Luc Godard: Seeing the Invisible*. Cambridge: Cambridge University Press.

7 Of totalitarianism and toilet doors

Alphaville does not, at first, appear like a film or a place, where arseholes, scum and shit might sound out. After all, the disembodied tones of supercomputer Alpha 60 run this town, whilst the women of Alphaville are typically branded, on occasion boxed up, and always stiltedly, subserviently and circularly scripted: *I'm very well, thank you, you're welcome* (Silverman and Farocki 1998, 62). Set in some dystopic future, *Alphaville*, although unmistakably a sci-fi film, is also unmistakably grounded in the pavements of 1960s Paris. Through a chiaroscuro comprised of streetlights and night sky, the City of Light time travels. In this way, *Alphaville* pushes cinema's real compositions to an extreme, 'creat[ing] the future from the present [...] constructing Alphaville from Paris' (Darke 2005, 66), and this realness further complicates cinematic temporality, for increasingly 'this futuristic city is also a throwback to the past; Godard conjures it, with metaphoric smoke and mirrors, out of Paris of the mid-1960s' (Silverman and Farocki 1998, 66). This time travel subtly hyperbolises the 'American-style modernization' (Betz 2009, 52) that Kristin Ross (1996) argues screened out (Sharpe 2020) the crimes of empire and creates an apparently playful palimpsest that seams the past, present and future of its urban urtext. Yet all is not as it seems, and, like love, tenderness, crying, consciousness and why, Camille's litany would likely end up on the city's ever-expanding list of words expunged from a frequently reissued dictionary that proscribes what citizens can say, think and feel. Whatever disappears from this organ of the State disappears from human consciousness and behaviour.

On occasion, Godard marries this 'Alpha-speech' (Silverman and Farocki 1998, 62), effectively a Newspeak *à la française*, with the film's ambiguous attitude towards 'the architectural modernity of 1960s Paris' (Schmid 2019, 132) that it bastardises when HLMs (*habitation à loyer modéré*/low-income housing) are mocked up as hospitals for citizens who resist the regime. Emblematic of the linguistic and civic clean-up that characterises Alphaville's totalitarianism, as well as broader discourses around hygiene that entail the *État*

(State) acting as verbal and municipal *égout* (sewer) (Laporte 2000 [1978], 56) by, for instance, banishing shit and ornament from French pavements and pages, respectively, here this Alpha-speech inadvertently forges a further palimpsest that once again seams the past, present and future: because like the world depicted in *Alphaville*, in the world of the film's production what could be said out loud was restrictive and restricted.

The original ban on *Le Petit Soldat* (1960) epitomises such censorship. Mythologisation and France's Ministry of Information fostered this omertà through purification and prohibition (see Sharpe 2017a, 130), and both would be at home in the world of *Alphaville*. Yet this isn't Alphaville, or Chinatown, it is 1960s France, where the distinct but interrelated hygienic imaginaries of myth, modern plumbing and memory circulate and contend with multiple regimes of repression. These imaginaries coalesce in the hygienic imaginary that euphemistically placed the 'dirty war', the Algerian War of Independence, into sharp relief with the rapid modernisation that France underwent during this period, and which coded the conflict as an act 'of violent housecleaning' (Ross 1996, 108). *Alphaville* thus chronicles not one but two worlds flush with ideology, and it does so by means of a 'palimpsestic structure' (Silverman 2013, 4) that encompasses books, bodies and bathrooms; prismatically channels unhygienic 'zones' (Greene 1999, 6) of French history and brings the film into dialogue with recent work on postcolonialism, decolonisation and memorialisation. Such a reading, which this chapter will pursue, integrates the film's hallmark chiaroscuro into the long shadow cast by the Algerian War, which continued to grow long after its initial release.

While the business of myth is to talk about things, so that 'it purifies them' (Barthes 1972 [1957], 143), and for centuries the French language has allowed extensive chatter about effluence (see Kim 2022), it has not been so effusive when it comes to State crimes and colonialism, and their respective legacies. Words necessary to the statement of 'pure' facts—apparently so prized by the hygienic imaginary of myth, for example, curfew, genocide, massacre, torture and war—were as outlawed as the robin redbreast is in Alphaville and only belatedly permitted (see Greene 1999, 133; Brozgal 2020). Accordingly, whatever disappears from the State vernacular disappears from the State record. The 17 October 1961 massacre is perhaps the most remarkable example of such laundering, variously achieved by State suppression, selective commemoration and self-censorship (see House and MacMaster 2006; Brozgal 2020; Sharpe 2020), which denied the massacre any 'commemorative autonomy of its own' (House and MacMaster 2006, 254). *Alphaville*, however, permits such autonomy, whereby interpreting the colonisation of speech by the authoritarian Alpha 60 as a tacit avowal of the crimes of empire no longer appears fanciful. Rather, the censorious environment of 1960s France reads as clear inspiration.

Alphaville is far from the first, or only, French New Wave film that masquerades history. Alain Resnais's *Nuit et brouillard* (1956)—of which, Philip Watts claims, '[t]he importance [...] for Godard cannot be overstated' (2010, 141)—is routinely cited as an allegory for the Algerian War (Dine 1994, 223; Silverman 2013, 29; Sharpe 2020, 12), whilst his later *Muriel ou le Temps d'un retour* (1963) miniaturises this mask and channels these traces of traumatic zones of French history into the everyday objects that fill Hélène's shop and the lives of its characters, for instance, tables, film projects and cigarettes (Greene 1999, 34; Ezra 2010, 189–90; Silverman 2013, 59–60). *Alphaville* thus joins 'the larger dynamic of disguise that New Wave directors used in order to represent unpalatable events both past and present' (Ezra 2010, 179), placing Godard amongst the filmmakers who, since the 1960s, have 'played an important role in shattering [...] hegemonic vision[s] of the national past' (Greene 1999, 7). Here the film image is the ultimate trace object, and its plasticity enables alternative memory models that are 'productive and not privative' (Rothberg 2009, 3). In the multidirectional model, memory is 'subject to ongoing negotiation, cross-referencing, and borrowing' (3) through the connections it forms between different historical events on-screen and on the page, while the palimpsestic model involves 'a ceaseless process of straddling and superimposition of elements, and condensation and displacement of meaning' (Silverman 2013, 22) 'whereby one element is seen through and transformed by another' (4). Curiously, the strategies engaged by these models reflect broader tendencies to 'layer over' (House and MacMaster 2006, 255), and cover up, unsanitary historical episodes, such as the 17 October 1961 massacre.

Alphaville constructs a similar palimpsest, which at first appears innocently Godardian, and existing responses to the film highlight its vestigial structure. For Chris Darke, 'every element of [Godard's] films' fabric is layered like a palimpsest. The choice of black and white film [...] has a host of connotations, as does the casting and the use of certain genres' (2005, 11). Marion Schmid argues that *Alphaville*'s 'supremely discreet' (2019, 38) scene of lovemaking marries the stylistic arsenal of cinema with Paul Éluard's poetry, and 'palimpsestically recalls its [dual] origins'. This structure, moreover, initially emerges as safely couched in references to the Second World War, or safer still, following one of the symptoms of Vichy syndrome, *résistancialisme* (Rousso 1991), to Nazi Germany. For instance, 'the "haunted" light of German expressionism' (Darke 2005, 41), the numbers tattooed on the women of Alphaville, the evil Professor von Braun, whose real-world Nazi rocket scientist namesake Wernher von Braun helped America keep up in the space race, as well as more discreet elements of its *mise en scène*. This is especially the case during Lemmy Caution's (Eddie Constantine) outing with the executive class of *Alphaville*, such as the 'SS' lift button captured in close-up that signifies *sous-sol* and denotes basement, but undoubtedly gestures elsewhere (see also Darke 2005, 76–7), and the swimming pool where the city's executions take place. In a faint allusion to the lines of people that score Holocaust imagery of round-ups, deportations and camps, men wait in line for their sentence. A burst of machine gunfire tips those convicted of illogical behaviour into the water where they are then finished off by a team of synchronised swimmers (another 'SS', albeit only when anglicised) armed with knives. This occasionally farcical scene, however, subtly shifts its ire from the safety of Nazism and Vichy to French complicity and Algeria through a deft auto-palimpsest that not only time travels but strips away the cleansing myth of *résistancialisme*. Yet it is not Godard's camera that does so, but Caution's, which alongside his trilby, Mac, and gun makes up an integral part of his private eye getup. His camera not only pastiches his *noir* origins but Bruno Forestier's hobby in *Le Petit Soldat*. Bruno's photography, of course, fell victim to censorship. Nonetheless, his encounter with Veronica (Anna Karina) is one of the most enduring sequences of the French New Wave. Here, Bruno and Veronica intermittently imitate Godard's first New Wave couple, Michel and Patricia, via a playful iris—achieved by a record sleeve—and talk of former boyfriends, although, unlike William Faulkner, significant cultural figures such as Bach, Beethoven, Haydn, Klee and Mozart are not mistaken for ex-lovers. This scene also establishes this duo's frequent chatter about personal hygiene which parallels the film's starker correspondences between hygiene and torture and, oddly, bibliophilia. During one torture scene, Bruno's captors read Simone de Beauvoir and Gisèle Halimi's book on Djamila Boupacha (1962) to him. Caution's camera thus smuggles *Le Petit Soldat*, and its explicit concern for the Algerian War, into *Alphaville* through the back door, which, fittingly, and in something of an architectural curiosity, leads through the bathroom and into room 344 at the Hotel Scribe where Caution is staying. In doing so, Caution's photography counters the iconoclasm of the censors by bearing witness to the watery grave to which State violence condemned citizens.

State-sanctioned murder and stadia have an ignoble place in twentieth-century French history. Between 16 and 17 July 1942, French police rounded up 13,000 Jewish men, women and children from across Paris and around 7000 were sent to the Vél d'Hiv stadium before being sent to their deaths at Auschwitz (Holocaust Encyclopedia n.d.). Having been used in the largest French deportation of Jews during the Holocaust, the Vél d'Hiv was later used to intern Algerians as part of the racist policies pursued by Maurice Papon, the préfect of police in Paris, which led to the 17 October 1961 massacre. Bodies shot and thrown into a body of water bring the massacre closer still because on 17 October 1961, and in the days that followed, between thirty-five and two hundred Algerians were thrown into the Seine by French police. No official record of the number of victims exists but Godard's oblique references to them here, variously repackaged by genre and *mise en scène*, unequivocally cast them as victims of State violence. Consequently, *Alphaville* enters what Lia Brozgal terms the anarchive, a 'rogue collection of cultural texts' (2020, 5) that remembers what history attempts to forget. Periodising the anarchive into three waves—1961–63, 1983–99 and 1999 and beyond—Brozgal maps its almost two decades of silence onto the prevailing 'political zeitgeist and absence of public discourse' (40) around the events of 17 October 1961. By means of a subterranean swimming pool, however, *Alphaville* extends the first wave and suggests that, like a synchronised swimmer assassin, repressed memories can only go so deep.

This centring of La Seine brings another of the earliest contributions to the anarchive into conjunction with *Alphaville*: Jacques Panijel's *Octobre à Paris* (1962). Banned until 1973, Panijel's film is celebrated for its portrayal of Algerian subjectivity. However, it is also criticised for its ending, which seizes the discourse and collapses the Charonne massacre, during which nine protestors were killed by police at the eponymous Métro station on 8 February 1962, onto 17 October, compromising the specificity of the film's address (Sharpe 2017b, 366–7; Brozgal 2020). These opposing positionalities can be mapped onto the film's relationship to embodiment. Panijel's disembodied voice, heard at the film's close, disenfranchises his erstwhile collaborators, whilst in its earliest moments *'Octobre à Paris* represents the river in a fashion that is distinctly interested in Algerians' embodied experiences […] turning the camera into a drowning victim' (Brozgal 2020, 186). *Alphaville* never gets that close to its drowning victims, but this acute sense of embodiment returns when the film signals its greatest solidarity.

Missing from the above-mentioned memory models, of course, are visions of the future, which our retrospection liberates. These visions once more draw *Alphaville* into the anarchive through its proximity to the 'pulpy trappings' (Brozgal 2020, 43) of the *polar*, which constitutes 'a crossover genre, moving from wave to wave' (53) and 'is imbued with the power to "smuggle truth past the guardians"' (43). Caution's camera realises such smuggling, whilst smuggling also coordinates the film's relationship between books, bodies and bathrooms. When Caution finally tracks down his missing colleague Henri Dickson (Akim Tamiroff) to the seedy Red Star Hotel, the latter laments the lack of art in the world that Alpha 60 has built and then greets the seductress who arrives mid-debrief with a litany of sobriquets—Mesdames Bovary, La Fayette, Pompadour, Récamier—that weave literature and sanitation together through their proximity to bastions of French culture and notoriety: the insalubrity of its court and palaces (see Spawforth 2008; Herman 2019). A site of seduction, secrets and death, Dickson's hotel room fulfils its generic promise (Silverman and Farocki 1998, 62), perhaps inaugurating the anarchive's relationship to detective fiction, and before expiring, Caution's comrade slips him a copy of Paul Éluard's *Capitale de la douleur* (1926), which will reappear during one of the film's trips to the bathroom.

Alphaville plays the prophet once again following Caution's first audience with Alpha 60. Interrogated by the disembodied dictator, Caution is then given a tour of its nerve centre which concludes with a prescient voice-over declaration that he doesn't need anyone to draw him a picture to understand Alpha 60's diabolic plan. He can draw his own map, and he does so via a montage that charts the regime's favoured architecture—circles and straight lines—and methods: assimilation, execution and invasion. His map, however, includes rebellious elements: images of Natasha von Braun (Anna Karina), images of love, perhaps as evidence of his resistance to the regime. A strange sanitary incantation, *occupé, libre, occupé, libre*, scores his corridor walks, whilst the white lab coat-clad apparatchiks who populate these scenes anticipate the prevalence of maps, and 'the colonial technology of cartography' (Brozgal 2020, 131), amongst the anarchive, most notably, the *renseignement généraux* sequence in Yasmina Adi's documentary *Ici on noie les Algériens* (2001) (133–6). Here, archival audio-visual footage creates an impression of sci-fi surveillance that was all too real for those protesting on 17 October. Yet, as Brozgal details, the recurrence of maps in the anarchive subtly erodes the control and knowledge they symbolise, including via the affect and embodiment that a hand-drawn map epitomises in *Mémoires du 17 octobre 1961* (Bernard Richard and Faïza Guène, 2002) (131–2). This erosion mirrors one of this book's principal critical concerns whereby defiant bodies and body parts disrupt textual systems, as well as Caution's cartographic confidence. Significantly, these anarchival maps recuperate Alphaville's architectural circles and lines, shapes that make up a basic bolt lock mechanism such as we might find on a toilet door. Considering Alpha 60's water closet chant, this is by no means a far-fetched transposition, and this starched iconography repeats later in the film when Caution takes out evil mastermind Professor von Braun. No longer manning the machines that power Alphaville, the city and its citizens collapse, exposing just how flimsy its totalitarian regime is. Alpha 60 is, after all, made from humble car parts, and its regime turns out to be no more robust than a lock on a toilet door: *occupé, libre, occupé, libre*.

Further echoes of the bathroom neighbour perhaps the film's most striking clairvoyance. *Alphaville* opens with a close-up shot of a frenetically flickering light, in the distinctive way that bathroom lights do, and two images appear on screen. The first shows a man walking beneath a mural that depicts a group pushing a tank off a jetty. Thanks to a pan up that resembles filmstock moving through a projector, a mural of two hands releasing a dove replaces the original composition. A tank, a dove, war, peace (Figures 7.1 and 7.2). If attuned to *Alphaville* as an anarchival witness, this short montage readily gives up its secrets. It quite literally spotlights the context that its palimpsest secretes. But it also stages the film's remarkable relationship to the future. By exposing the stillness that underpins all film images, *Alphaville* here takes care of

Of totalitarianism and toilet doors 69

Figure 7.1 Visions of the past, present and future: War.

Figure 7.2 Visions of the past, present and future: Peace.

the present and pays a fleeting homage to Chris Marker's precious *photo-roman La jetée* (1962). The painted jetty accentuates this interpersonal paean. Significantly, the film's tribute does not end with reverential citation because the inadvertent indiscretion of these images is indirectly performed by Marker; these two images are in fact one photograph taken by Godard's contemporary in Moscow sometime between 1957 and 1960 (Darke 2005, 86). Marker was unaware of their inclusion in *Alphaville* until he saw the film and later 'reclaimed' the photograph in *Immemory* (1997)—its cutting-edge CD-ROM format a testament to the telescoping of futurity. Remarkably, this belated reintegration, and some of the responses it inspired, draws on a familiar vernacular. Godard's film 'becomes a (cinema) screen within the (computer) screen on which Marker replays the credit sequence of *Alphaville*', whilst for Raymond Bellour 'We are before a collage with many levels of meaning and sensation' (quoted in Darke 2005, 87). Equally remarkably, even decades after the massacre, these screens incidentally insulate *Alphaville* from suspicion. For, as Brozgal summarises: 'it was only in 1999, that is, 37 years after independence, that the "police operations" or "events" in Algeria were officially recognized as a "war"' (2020, 13). These screens, however, point towards, rather than away from, *Alphaville*'s secrets, much like its relationship to books, which also returns us to the bathroom.

Alpha 60 parroting a toilet door indicates that even totalitarianism needs the odd toilet break. Indeed, totalitarianism and toilets are more intimately aligned than we might think, and when totalitarianism speaks these links reify: 'Methodically collect your manure and give it to the State that wishes you well. Give up this shit, this fruit of your labor, and in return, I will fulfill all your needs' (Laporte 2000 [1978], 129). Our bodily evacuations, moreover, constitute its fundament: 'Totalitarianism simply involves [...] the relegation of shit to the private realm' (66). This relegation of shit to the private realm is part and parcel of a centuries-long narrative that Dominique Laporte documents in the idiosyncratic *History of Shit* (2000 [1978]), and 'along with others, serves as a reference point for the inception of the modern State' (66). Key to its conception was the domestication (28), privatisation and individuation of waste (65) initiated by a sixteenth-century edict that ordered Parisian citizens to shut themselves up with their own shit. The street was no longer to serve as the city's sewer, and instead the home inherited this stercorary responsibility. For Laporte, this shift 'must certainly have played a role in the emergence of the family and familial intimacy' (28) and 'prefigured, not so insignificantly perhaps, the Cartesian ideology of the *I*' (30–1). My shit stinks therefore I am.

Such an ideology scents the French New Wave's men's room, which, like the politics of waste that started in the sixteenth century, is equally fragrant with repression. In the context of the French New Wave, this repression concerns literature, specifically 'literature *qua* adaptation' (Kline 1992, 3), in which the Cartesian ideology of the *I* finds another expression despite the fact that written language, as Barthes reminds us, is inherently fragrance-free (Laporte 2000 [1978], 18). In the annals of the French cultural imaginary, books are a 'prized, foundational element of [...] identity' (3) with the 'radical difference' of French autobiographical writing from its Anglophone equivalent accounted for due to the former's 'substitution of the *bibliothèque* for the *berceau* ("cradle")' (2). Parenting such privatised representations in the masculine singular—T. Jefferson Kline lists Montaigne, Rousseau, Stendhal and Sartre as examples of this literary distinction—puts paid to the lie of another prized, foundational element of French identity, the stench of abstract universalism, which the French New Wave reinforces through its ideology of auteurism, as well as the *I* of the cinephilic texts written by its contemporary proponents and its 'uncomplicated expression of a masculine subjectivity that considers itself universal' (Sellier 2008, 29). This writing testifies to Kline's reminder that whatever gets repressed has an 'uncanny way of returning in another form' (3), and, according to Kline, this return took the form of 'self-conscious theorizing', 'usurping the place of the writer' (4) and an 'obsession with the book'. The French New Wave's typical androcentrism, both on- and off-screen, thus attests to 'repression's sublimated return' (Laporte 2000 [1978], 27). Alongside usurpation and obsession, books in French New Wave films typically screen things out 'in the sense that Freud gave to the term, as a memory "behind which lies a submerged and forgotten" phrase, event, or, [...] text' (Kline 1992, 4). In *Alphaville*, however, books signal the truth and operate as a dual rejoinder to the New Wave's literary repression and to the deferrals, displacements and deceptions that personal, collective and official memory enacts.

The book in question is Éluard's *Capitale de la douleur*, which, having been smuggled to Caution by Dickson, then reappears in another lengthy domestic sequence bookended by the bathroom, where it dominates. Its reappearance here shores up the bathroom's generic contours as all manner of rogues and henchmen pass through it and transforms the bathroom into a secret agent that conspires against the hygienic imaginary of Alphaville. Perhaps sensing that something is amiss, Alphaville sends a lackey, played by Jean-Pierre Léaud, to room 344, and he distributes the latest version of the city's dictionary. Whilst not a French New Wave cascade as seen in *Une femme est une femme* (1961) and *Masculin féminin* (1966), it does suggest a systemic vulnerability that such influxes connote elsewhere; although here it is the film world, rather than the auteur, that experiences this threat to control—a shift in vulnerability that anticipates the shift in systemic Godardian political action.[1] Unfamiliar with Éluard's work, and even poetry, Natasha soon pens her own love poem and in a post-coitus close-up is pictured at the window with Éluard's tome in hand. The shot is a stunning palimpsest with Natasha, Alphaville and the book's cover superimposed on the glass (Figure 7.3). This palimpsest gets denser still if we

72 *Of totalitarianism and toilet doors*

Figure 7.3 Postcolonial palimpsest.

superimpose Éluard's poetry onto it, which we hear earlier in the scene when Natasha and Caution read brief extracts, and experience it in a remarkably embodied way, thanks to a point-of-view shot that shows Natasha reading 'La nudité de la vérité'. Her eyes skim the page and linger on certain words— *nudité* (nudity), *ailes* (wings), *amour* (love)—and in a speculative leafing through of the collection they could also dart towards the second stanza of 'Les Petits Justes', another 'winged' poem, where language asks: 'why am I beautiful? / Because my master bathes me'. Disclosing the workings of the hygienic imaginary of totalitarianism, whilst utilising words outlawed by Alphaspeech, such talk confirms Alpha 60's authority because it bathes language—a clean-up that echoes the hygienic imaginary of myth—and these lines preface Laporte's *History of Shit*. However, here *Alphaville* rejects any such cleansing imaginary and instead shines a disinfecting light on the state apparatus, which, unusually for a French New Wave film, results in literary revelation. Although couched in the apparent safety of collage, the first extract we hear, 'Nous vivons dans l'oubli de nos métamorphoses', initiates this disclosure, for it originates in an earlier Éluard tome, *Le dur désir de durer* (1950), which also opens Jacques Doniol-Valcroze's *La Dénonciation* (1962)—another French New Wave film, alongside *Le Petit Soldat,* that covers the activities of the OAS *(Organisation Armée Secrète*/Secret Armed Organisation*)*. The rehearsal of this line expresses, or reveals, solidarity with Doniol-Valcroze, whilst thoughts of Éluard's earlier collaboration with Alain Resnais on *Guernica* (1950) thicken this warring collage, and this palimpsest houses another vision from the future, this time by hijacking rather than smuggling.

Such a rhetorical '*détournement*' foretells a moment in Rachid Bouchareb's *Hors-la-loi* (2010), in which Abdelkader, one of the brothers the film follows, tells those gathered for the peaceful protest on 17 October 1961: 'Pour un coup reçu, nous en porterons dix' (For every blow received, we will dole out ten) (see Brozgal 2020, 291). These words were originally spoken by Papon, and Abdelkader's 'recuperation' (292) of them 'appropriat[es] Papon's power and reinvest[s] the threat with new meaning'. In wielding Éluard's tome, Natasha wields the hygienic imaginary of totalitarianism against it, thanks to her stubborn corporeality, which the film literalises first by her insurgent tears, batheing her cheeks instead of language, when Caution is whisked away to Alpha 60's nerve centre, then by reading poetry, and finally by loving Caution. In holding the hygienic imaginary in her hands, Natasha becomes politically *engagé* and essentially collaborates with Caution in the literary overthrowing of the regime, stemming Godard's usual disenfranchisement of female characters.

The subtle encounters between books, bodies and bathrooms thus transform *Alphaville* into a postcolonial palimpsest, which resignifies Lemmy Caution and transitions him from secret agent to surprise *appelé*, and which in turn reconfigures the strangeness of life in the technocratic Alphaville. His disorientation and multiple beatings stand in for 'the painful reinsertion of the traumatized members of the contingent into a rapidly modernizing society' (Dine 1994, 221). The bureaucratic stonewalling and circular speech he must contend with resonates with the 'uneasy, embarrassed silence' (Greene 1999, 134) that 'greeted' veterans upon their return from 'a war "without a name"' (see also Stora 1991). The extremes created by its lighting design accent the modernisation that defined the era but, in this instance, they do not screen out the violent housekeeping that the contemporary fixation on modernisation conventionally, and conveniently, sought to displace. Rather, they surreptitiously superimpose it onto the strange adventure of Lemmy Caution.[2] Caution's over-inscription thus places *Alphaville* in solidarity with the filmmakers and films silenced by censorship, whether activist or *appelé*, for example, *Le combat dans l'île* (Alain Cavalier, 1962) and *La Belle vie* (Robert Enrico, 1963), and holds space for memories considered ideologically unhygienic.

Notes

1 In the later *Deux ou trois choses que je sais d'elle* and *La Chinoise* (both 1967), references to Algeria are bolder and take the form of a poster for Alain Resnais's

Muriel ou le temps d'un retour (1963) on a wall in the former and the inclusion of Francis Jeanson, a renowned political activist who worked for Algerian independence, among the cast of the latter. There is also a mention of Charonne in *Made in USA* (1966).

2 See Sharpe (2017a) for another use of superimposition in *appelé* cinema (133).

References

Barthes, Roland. 1972 [1957]. *Mythologies*. Translated by Annette Lavers. New York: Farrar, Strauss & Giroux.
Betz, Mark. 2009. *Beyond the Subtitle: Remapping European Cinema*. Minneapolis: University of Minnesota Press.
Brozgal, Lia. 2020. *Absent the Archive: Cultural Traces of a Massacre in Paris, 17 October 1961*. Liverpool: Liverpool University Press.
Darke, Chris. 2005. *Alphaville*. London: I.B. Tauris.
Dine, Philip. 1994. *Images of the Algerian War: French Fiction and Film, 1954–1992*. Oxford: Oxford University Press.
Ezra, Elizabeth. 2010. "Cléo's Masks: Regimes of Objectification in the French New Wave." *Yale French Studies* 118/119: 177–190
Greene, Naomi. 1999. *Landscapes of Loss: The National Past in Postwar French Cinema*. Princeton: Princeton University Press.
Herman, Eleanor. 2019. *The Royal Art of Poison: Fatal Cosmetics, Deadly Medicines and Murder Most Foul*. Richmond: Duckworth.
Holocaust Encyclopedia. n.d. "The Vélodrome d'Hiver (Vél d'Hiv) Roundup." <https://encyclopedia.ushmm.org/content/en/article/the-velodrome-dhiver-vel-dhiv-roundup>
House, Jim and Neil MacMaster. 2006. *Paris 1961: Algerians, State Terror, and Memory*. Oxford: Oxford University Press.
Kim, Annabel L. 2022. *Cacaphonies: The Excremental Canon of French Literature*. Minneapolis: University of Minnesota Press.
Kline, T. Jefferson. 1992. *Screening the Text: Intertextuality in French New Wave Cinema*. Baltimore: The Johns Hopkins University Press.
Laporte, Dominique. 2000 [1978]. *History of Shit*. Translated by Nadia Benabid and Rodolphe el-Khour. Cambridge, MA: The MIT Press.
Ross, Kristin. 1996. *Fast Cars, Clean Bodies: Decolonization and the Reordering of French Culture*. Cambridge, MA: The MIT Press.
Rothberg, Michael. 2009. *Multidirectional Memory: Remembering the Holocaust in the Age of Decolonization*. Stanford: Stanford University Press.
Rousso, Henry. 1991. *The Vichy Syndrome: History and Memory in France since 1944*. Translated by Arthur Goldhammer. Cambridge, MA: Harvard University Press.
Schmid, Marion. 2019. *Intermedial Dialogues: The French New Wave and the Other Arts*. Edinburgh: Edinburgh University Press.
Sellier, Geneviève. 2008. *Masculine Singular: French New Wave Cinema*. Translated by Kristin Ross. Durham: Duke University Press.
Sharpe, Mani. 2020. "Tracing the Shadows of Occupation: Memory as 'screen' in *La Dénonciation* (1962) and *Tu ne tueras point* (1961/1963)." *Modern & Contemporary France* 28 (1): 1–17.

Sharpe, Mani. 2017a. "Screening Decolonisation through Privatisation in Two New Wave Films: *Adieu Philippine* and *La Belle Vie*." *French Cinema* 17 (2): 129–43.

Sharpe, Mani. 2017b. "Visibility, Speech and Disembodiment in Jacques Panijel's *Octobre à Paris*." *French Cultural Studies* 28 (4): 360–70.

Silverman, Kaja and Harun Farocki. 1998. *Speaking about Godard*. New York: New York University Press.

Silverman, Max. 2013. *Palimpsestic Memory: The Holocaust and Colonialism in French and Francophone Fiction and Film*. New York: Berghahn Books.

Spawforth, Tony. 2008. *Versailles: A Biography of a Palace*. New York: St Martin's Press.

Stora, Benjamin. 1991. *La gangrène et l'oubli. La mémoire de la guerre d'Algérie*. Paris: La Découverte.

Watts, Philip. 2010. "Godard's Wars." *L'Esprit Créateur* 50 (4): 137–149.

8 Conclusion

This book's focus on bodies, books and bathrooms in Jean-Luc Godard's New Wave films responds in part, I hope, to Roland-François Lack's call to action that work be done on the 'stopping places' (2018, 66) that feature in French New Wave films. Listing corridors, lifts, staircases, windows, balconies and bedrooms (74) as such *lieux de repos*, the bathroom, and its verbal agenda, is undoubtedly such a place, and the characters encountered across these pages take advantage of the downtime that it admits. Equally, the bathroom houses the movement that inheres in corridors, lifts and staircases, through the leisurely activities protagonists carry out there, and the elsewhere onto which windows, balconies and bedrooms open, even if only in dreams. Sometimes the bathroom opens onto bedrooms, at times doubling down on the immobility such *lieux* cultivate (*À bout de souffle* [1960], *Une femme mariée* [1964], *Deux ou trois choses que je sais d'elle* [1967]). Sometimes it opens onto corridors that allow all sorts, such as colleagues, flatmates, spouses and meter readers, to wander into it (*Le Mépris* [1963], *Alphaville* [1965], *Masculin féminin* [1966], *Deux ou trois choses que je sais d'elle*). Comings and goings that permit an alternative lens for tracking Godard's increasing contempt for narrative cinema and the Americanisation of everyday life through the metaphorical decline that the bathroom undergoes across his New Wave period: from a site of generic and romantic play to a space invaded by inspectors, US imperialism and cannibals. Arguably, then, in Godard's New Wave films, the bathroom anchors an entire network of *lieux de repos*.

Books embody a similar sense of stillness and movement. They are used as sunscreen (*Le Mépris*), forts (*Deux ou trois choses que je sais d'elle*, *La Chinoise* [1967]), ideological weapons (*Le Petit Soldat* [1960], *Alphaville*, *La Chinoise*) and lubricants for ambition (*Pierrot le fou* [1965]), flirtation (*À bout de souffle*, *Le Petit Soldat*, *Une femme mariée*) and rage (*Une femme est une femme* [1962], *Le Mépris*). Books also get characters moving as they shop for their next tome, and such episodes channel the ambiguity of the bookshop in relation to the street. Their open shopfronts and carousel stands skirt the pavement, making them satellites of it, yet belong to private commercial spaces. Public conveniences channel a similar ambiguity via vespasiennes (Figure 8.1).

DOI: 10.4324/9781003276241-8

Conclusion 77

Figure 8.1 A vespasienne in *Masculin féminin* (1966).

Godard's New Wave characters, however, largely benefit from private water closets which, like the female bodies that occupy them, emerge as rebellious sites, for at times they gesture towards the unsayable, and consequently stray into the censorious. Sometimes they get caught, their distribution shorted. Sometimes they don't. In such instances, the body acts as a vehicle for State violence. In other instances, it is a conduit for '(French) Theory', perhaps producing its necessary 'turd' (Fink 2004, 66)—that 'discrete, discernible object [...] for us to examine (admire or scorn)'—and perhaps succeeding where literature fails in approaching the concrete universalism for which Annabel L. Kim advocates (2022, 3):

> Fecality provides the opportunity to ground the universal in something that is concrete and corporeal, even to the point of revulsion. But as distasteful as fecality is for most, I would argue that it is the only form of corporeal universality and of universality tout court that we can accede to. Unlike human rights, fecality is truly universal. Everyone defecates.
>
> (26–7)

Even if shitting per se is rare in Godard's New Wave films and mistaken for the phallus when it does come up (*Week-end* [1967]), the recurrence of the bathroom is a discreet reminder that 'every body shits' (28) and of the very possibility of a 'fecal universalism'. The bathroom also acts as a space for subtle showdowns where women's bodies escape diegetic interiority, and while these resistant textures do not solve or surmount the contradictions of female embodiment in Godard's New Wave period, they do disrupt and denaturalise the gender dynamic commonly viewed as fundamental to it. Indeed, their fugitive status stages solace and solidarity, which his most embodied New Wave film, *Une femme mariée*, emblematises.

Charting one woman's relationship with her husband and lover, the film obsessively enumerates women's bodies, including that of Charlotte, its lead protagonist, via shots of body parts pictured in isolation, and a lengthy sequence that sets a litany of bra adverts to music. The bathroom contributes to this sense of embodiment: on a first visit, Charlotte attempts to measure herself for a bra, and during a second trip, she bathes and trims her body hair but not before her legs are imaged in isolation. Presented in bits, Charlotte's body initially appears like an object lesson in 'to-be-looked-at-ness' (see Mulvey 1975). This seemingly endless flow of body parts, and bras, risks constituting yet more exhibits for Godard's imaginary museum of female degradation. However, paired with the preponderance of caresses and backs that recur in *Une femme mariée*, which digitally and dorsally articulate authorial/masculine vulnerability and female kinship, what is actually secreted among this risky structure is the agency that the appropriative, disruptive and resistive opacity of women's bodies possesses. When torn from the diegesis, and apparently torn apart, Charlotte's face, back and limbs do not become new museum pieces, but rather reflect her refusal to give all of herself to her lovers. The film's circularity, opening and closing with the same image of Charlotte's outstretched left arm on white bedding, echoes this refusal, for it implies impenetrability (opacity) and interchangeability (Pierre? Robert? Who cares?), which the bathroom endorses. On two occasions, we see Charlotte washing her hands with her lovers, and whilst the film makes clear that she is willing to share soap with these men, its whispered voice-over, which further fleshes out Charlotte, thanks to the 'whole carnal stereophony' (Barthes 1998 [1973], 66) that the 'grain' of her voice conjures, suggests that she holds back significant pieces of herself, however compulsively the film screens her body—sometimes entangled with her lovers' bodies in an echo of Agnès Varda's knotted New Wave corporeality (Figures 8.2 and 8.3). Her corporeality thus serves as the film's architecture, and we might extend its adhesion to the French New Wave writ large because despite what little may in fact unite its films and directors, it is undoubtedly bound by bodies that transcend both sides of the Seine. Bodily matter produces, even anchors, French New Wave cinema.

Finally, the bathroom in Godard's New Wave films might just be the best place to be because, overwhelmingly, Godardian cinema during this period is not a safe space for the body. Bodies are beaten (*Alphaville*, *La Chinoise*), shot dead (*À bout de souffle*, *Vivre sa vie* [1962], *Les Carabiniers* [1963], *Bande à Part* [1964], *Alphaville*, *Made in USA* [1966], *Week-end*), kidnapped

Conclusion 79

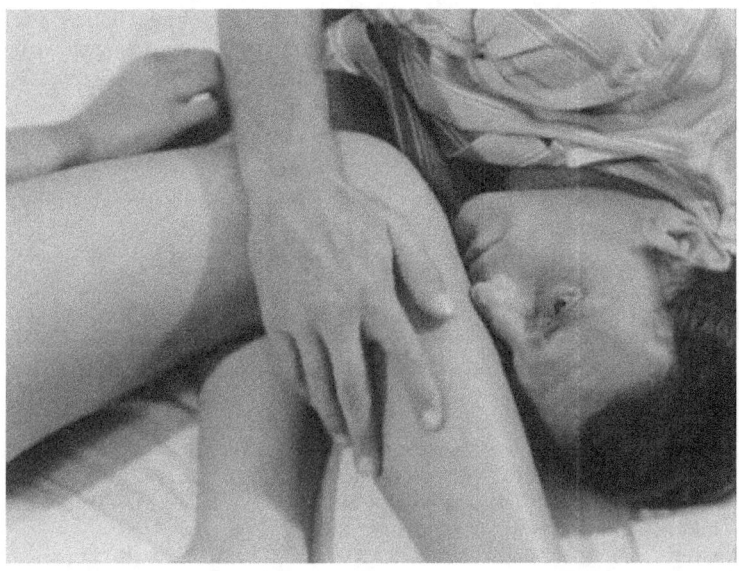

Figure 8.2 Godard's knotted French New Wave corporeality: *Une femme mariée* (1964).

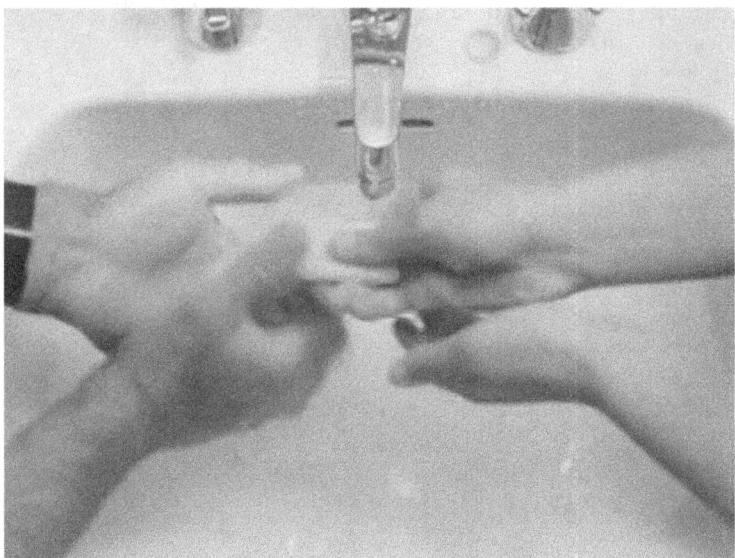

Figure 8.3 Sharing soap but not herself.

Conclusion

and tortured (*Le Petit Soldat, Pierrot le fou*), raped (*Week-end*), killed in car accidents (*Le Mépris, Week-end*), blown up or threatened with being blown up (*Pierrot le fou, La Chinoise*), defenestrated (*Masculin féminin*), cannibalised (*Week-end*), prostituted (*Vivre sa vie, La Chinoise, Deux ou trois choses que je sais d'elle*) and immolated (*Masculin féminin, Week-end*). Indeed, excepting *Made in USA*, stopping off in the bathroom seems like the best way to survive Godard's New Wave films, whilst, of course, causing a little disruption too.

References

Barthes, Roland. 1998 [1973]. *The Pleasure of the Text*. Translated by Richard Miller. New York: Hill and Wang.

Fink, Bruce. 2004. *Lacan to the Letter: Reading Ecrits Closely*. Saint Paul: University of Minnesota Press.

Kim, Annabel L. 2022. *Cacaphonies: The Excremental Canon of French Literature*, Minneapolis: University of Minnesota Press.

Lack, Roland-François. 2018. "The New Wave Hotel." In *Paris in the Cinema: Beyond the Flâneur*, edited by Alastair Phillips and Ginette Vincendeau, 66–75. London: BFI Palgrave.

Mulvey, Laura. 1975. "Visual Pleasure and Narrative Cinema." *Screen* 16 (3): 6–18.

Index

17 October 1961 64–8, 73

Algerian War of Independence 13, 34, 44, 64–6, 70
art cinema 1, 10–11, 49

Balázs, Béla 26, 49
Bardot, Brigitte 4, 8, 38, 53–5, 57, 60–1
Barthes, Roland 9, 15, 35–6, 71; myth 64, 72
Baudrillard, Jean 56
Bazin, André 13, 45–6
Belmondo, Jean-Paul 7, 13, 29, 31, 38, 41, 46, 48
Bouchareb, Rachid 73
Brialy, Jean-Claude 41

Cavalier, Alain 73
Chabrol, Claude 9
Charonne massacre 67
Chion, Michel 23

Deleuze, Gilles 7–9, 12, 15, 23, 26, 38
Doniol-Valcroze, Jacques 72–3
Douglas, Mary 22
Duras, Marguerite 46, 49–50

Éluard, Paul 65, 68, 71–3
Enrico, Robert 73
Epstein, Jean 12, 46

Gilles, Guy 34
Godard, Jean-Luc: À bout de souffle 4, 24–5, 29–41, 43–4, 46, 48, 55, 76, 78; Alphaville 24, 56, 63–76, 78; Bande à part 2–4, 15, 55, 78; Les Carabiniers 15–6, 78; La Chinoise 44, 76, 78, 80; Deux ou trois choses que je sais d'elle 25, 54, 56, 76, 80; Une femme est une femme 4, 24, 41–52, 55–6, 61, 71, 76; Une femme mariée 15, 49, 76, 78–9; Histoire(s) du cinéma 57; Made in USA 78, 80; Masculin féminin 4, 11, 26, 37–8, 43–4, 48, 71, 76–7, 80; Le Mépris 4, 8, 11, 24, 53–62, 76, 80; Le Petit Soldat 13–4, 55, 64, 66, 72, 76, 80; Pierrot le fou 4, 13–4, 38, 43, 55, 76, 80; Vivre sa vie 4, 26, 45–6, 49, 55–6, 78, 80; and Week-end 5, 11, 25, 54, 57–60, 77–8, 80

Italian Neorealism 1, 13, 45

Karina, Anna 3–4, 11, 15, 24, 41, 45–6, 55–7, 59, 66, 68

Lacan, Jacques 21, 29, 42–3
Léaud, Jean-Pierre 7, 26, 37–8, 71

Malle, Louis 10
Marker, Chris 70
Metz, Christian 20
Moreau, Jeanne 7, 10, 46, 48

Panijel, Jacques 67

résistancialisme 65–6
Resnais, Alain: Guernica 73; Hiroshima mon amour 49–50; Muriel ou le Temps d'un retour 65; and Nuit et brouillard 65
Rohmer, Éric 35

Seberg, Jean 4, 11
Subor, Michel 13, 55

Tati, Jacques 5
Truffaut, François 7, 26, 38, 46; *Les 400 coups* 38; *Baisers volés* 26; and *Jules et Jim* 7–8, 46

Varda, Agnès 2–4, 8, 22, 48–9, 78; *Le bonheur* 3–4; *Cléo de 5 à 7* 8, 22; *Les fiancés du pont Mac Donald* 5; *Lion's Love* 15; *L'Opéra-Mouffe* 3, 8, 43–5, 47–8; *La Pointe courte* 3; and *Visages, Villages* 2

For Product Safety Concerns and Information please contact our EU representative GPSR@taylorandfrancis.com
Taylor & Francis Verlag GmbH, Kaufingerstraße 24, 80331 München, Germany

www.ingramcontent.com/pod-product-compliance
Lightning Source LLC
Chambersburg PA
CBHW061959220426
43662CB00011B/1749